Both Feet on God's Path

Both Feet on God's Path

The Story of Julie Fehr

Lisa M. Rohrick

Christian Publications
Camp Hill, Pennsylvania

Christian Publications
3825 Hartzdale Drive, Camp Hill, PA 17011

Faithful, biblical publishing since 1883

ISBN: 0-87509-672-7
LOC Catalog Card: 96-83899

Printed in the United States of America

96 97 98 99 00 5 4 3 2 1
Cover Illustration by Karl Foster

Contents

Foreword

The shadows of the Central African rain forest where Julie Fehr spent the best years of her life are brightened by an astonishing variety of butterflies. They come in all sizes, all colors, all shapes. When they stop long enough for the eye to catch more than a blaze of color, you discover breathtaking patterns of light and color on their wings and bodies.

The more you look at these lovely creatures, the more you realize that each one is beautiful for different reasons. The enormous turquoise butterfly is startling for its size and color, but its wings do not match the beauty and intricacy of the more numerous tiny butterflies. When one of these fragile creatures pauses to settle on a sunlit leaf, slowly opening and closing its wings, one does not naturally remember that it was once an ugly caterpillar.

I was an intern at a hospital in San Diego hoping to become a missionary surgeon when Julie Fehr visited our church. She wore a flowing Gabonese dress on her slight frame that accentuated her natural grace. When she walked, the folds of her robe fluttered like wings.

Julie was at ease among complete strangers. I first noticed it when she stood in front of our church and spoke with great emotion about how much the people of Gabon needed to hear about the love of Jesus. I noticed it again three years later when I came to visit her church in the jungles of south Gabon. Like a butterfly who settles as easily on a clod of dirt as on a flower, Julie seemed to belong wherever God asked her to live and to do well whatever God asked her to do.

Among the primitive Tsogo people, she lived, spoke and even thought like a Tsogo. Years later when she moved to Gabon's capital, she lived, spoke and even thought like the educated, middle-class and upper-class Gabonese who she led to faith in Jesus Christ.

Julie's special color and hue was her ability to think and feel like those among whom she lived. Her God-given pattern was her unshaking belief that the Holy Spirit of God could enable African believers to do everything that Western believers and missionaries did, only better.

From these gifts and convictions flowed a vibrant translation of the New Testament into the Tsogo language, the evangelism and discipling of hundreds of Tsogo believers in remote villages, a successful ministry to middle- and upper-class Gabonese people in cities, a nationwide program of decentralized theological education that trained lay leaders for the church and, her final gift, a vision for French-speaking African churches to send missionaries to the unevangelized world.

Julie was neither the brightest or biggest butterfly in God's creation, but because she gave herself completely to God, He took a farm girl from Canada and fashioned a work of rare and wonderful beauty.

David C. Thompson, M.D.
January 1996

Preface

What a privilege to be the one to write Julie Fehr's story. Julie was a beautiful woman of God with exceptional giftedness and a joy in living that made her an asset to the Church worldwide.

Julie was also a close friend and mentor to me. It all started several years ago when my home church in Invermere, British Columbia, started an adopt-a-missionary program. My mother chose to adopt Julie because they shared the same birthday. Julie and I knew of each other only through the mail for a few years. Then, when she was home in Abbotsford and I was living nearby, we got together. During the next few years we made it a priority to visit every time Julie was on this continent, meeting in several different places.

In 1992 I had the opportunity to spend a month in Gabon, most of which I spent with Julie. I was there when her brother phoned at 5:30 a.m. to tell her that their mother had just died. Sharing that moment drew us even closer together.

Julie modeled Christ's love in her ministry, her day-to-day business and her play. She showed me how to minister effectively as a single woman. She gave me so much of herself—encouragement, counsel, instruction, humor and love. She was my mentor in life, but also my mentor in death—dying an ugly death in a beautiful way. As I have read through Julie's letters and journals these past months, and learned more of her heart, my love and respect for her has deepened.

In these pages I have tried to paint an accurate picture of Julie's life and ministry. There are many stories I had to leave out, but I trust the ones I chose will encourage you, make you laugh and challenge you to walk more closely with Julie's Jesus.

I have not been alone through this project. I wish to express my thanks to those who came alongside.

Thanks to Dr. Joan Carter and Rev. Gordon Fowler for encouraging me to start the project in the first place and for believing that I could do it.

A big thanks to Julie's brothers and sisters—Florence, Ken, Dolores, and Bernie—for making available over 1,500 letters Julie wrote home, as well as journals, photo albums, etc. Thank you for sharing your sister with me.

Thanks to my parents for putting up with letters and notes strewn from one end of your basement to another month after month. And thanks, Mom, for reading each chapter armed with a red pen as it came off the printer.

Thanks to Bev Arnold, John and Fran Corby, Ron and Joan Israel, Esther Lutzer, Ruth Parliman, Anita Reader, Dr. David Thompson and Kati Venneberg for proofreading and helping me get the story straight in correct English.

Thanks to Marilynne Foster for your gentle editing and helpful suggestions.

There are many others who have offered words of encouragement, prayed for me and given suggestions. You know who you are. Thank you.

Most of all I am thankful to Julie's Jesus, who is also my Jesus. Thanks for paying the price for sin and bringing new life—the message Julie dedicated her life to communicating to the Gabonese. Thank You for the promise of eternal life. Thank You for friends, and in particular, a treasured friendship with Julianna Rose Fehr.

1

Jars of Clay

Over 1,000 people gathered in a conference room of a Toronto hotel. It was June 21, the opening evening of the 1994 General Assembly of The Christian and Missionary Alliance in Canada. The theme of the conference heralded a powerful truth: "The Church—Chosen to Triumph." Julie Fehr stood behind the stage, waiting to tell of the triumphant church in Gabon, Equatorial Africa. At her cue, she stepped up to the microphone, looked toward an audience whom bright lights prevented her from seeing, and spoke these words:

> It was 1965. Rev. Donald Fairley, one of the founding missionaries of The Christian and Missionary Alliance in Gabon, Equatorial Africa, talked about his dreams and prayers for a church of blood-bought, spirit-anointed men and women.
>
> I was a brand-new missionary—so new that my hero worship of missionaries was still intact. I had

not been there long enough to discover that we have more than feet of clay. Our clay starts at the feet and goes all the way up. But we are redeemed clay. Christ has chosen to live in clay temples, and through them, build His church.

I listened as this heroic man, tears in his eyes, talked about new believers who slipped back into traditional religions. They could not withstand family and clan pressure or persecution. Then he told how he prayed and fasted before the Lord that the Church in Gabon might really take root as if it came from Gabonese soil itself, not a North American transplant.

The Fairleys retired. They left a legacy of faith and perseverance and the Church God established through their labor. Gabonese pastors, struggling converts and missionaries together continued the work of our founders, working with Christ, the Head of the Church. Week after week the Church grew—here an inch, there an inch—one hard-fought battle at a time. One redeemed life here, one redeemed life there. We celebrated with the angels in heaven.

But in between celebrations we mourned those who turned away. We agonized with those who struggled to catch their next spiritual breath in a polluted environment. At times the gospel seemed ineffective. The enemy appeared to be victorious.

Meanwhile we heard of winds of revival in neighboring Zaire and of uncontrollable church growth in Nigeria. Your missionaries looked at each other in the year 1978 and shook their heads, saying, "Maybe this wind of revival is like a whirlwind bouncing about; maybe we are in the vortex with our life being sucked out of us." You continued to pray. Your brothers and sisters in Gabon, national and missionary, kept working.

In 1979 I stood within the roofless walls of The Christian and Missionary Alliance's first permanent building in Libreville, the capital city. The builders excitedly told me it would seat 450! Four hundred and fifty in a Christian and Missionary Alliance church? In Libreville? At that time approximately 150 met in a portable chapel. I wondered if during my missionary career I would see that church building filled to capacity. What would that look like?

Five years later I was again standing within the walls of the Libreville sanctuary—standing this time because there was no seat! A side wall was knocked out of that five-year-old building and its capacity doubled. Within months there were overflow crowds again, setting up tent tarpaulins to provide shade. The other side wall was torn down and the original building size was tripled. Soon the tarpaulins went back up for a new overflow crowd. There was only one ordained pastor and several North American missionaries—each of us made of clay.

What happened? Donald Fairley's burden, his vision was being fulfilled. There were hundreds of committed Christians. They led their families, their colleagues at work and their neighbors to the Lord.

Twelve years after I had first stood in that building and wondered if I would in my lifetime see a 450-seat sanctuary filled, the Avea church began two morning services with more than 2,000 in each service. God is building His Church. He did so in the past. He continues to do so today. He has chosen to build it through you and me, vessels of clay that we are, for "we have this treasure in jars of clay to show that this all-surpassing power is from God and not from us" (2 Corinthians 4:7).

That was to be the last time Julie Fehr spoke in public. Less than a week later she was hospitalized and never released. Julie was a woman of clay—redeemed and gifted clay—lovingly crafted by the hands of the Master Potter. In her clay jar she carried a priceless treasure, the Holy Spirit of God, who used her to build His Church in Gabon and elsewhere.

Here is her story.

2

Make It Matter!

As spring came to the Canadian prairies, four young girls spent their lunch hour at an abandoned hockey rink adjacent to their one-room schoolhouse. It felt good to play in the warm spring air after a long, cold winter. Out of breath, they rested in the dressing room beside the rink. It was time for a serious discussion.

"Are you Christians?" Ruthie asked.

"No," replied the honest, eight-year-old Julie while the others listened in.

"If you ask Jesus to come into your heart, you can become one," Ruthie carefully explained. "Do you want to do that?"

The idea wasn't new to Julie. She had heard that invitation before. The middle of five children, she grew up on an isolated farm 68 kilometers (45 miles) from Saskatoon, Saskatchewan. Though they rarely attended church, Julie's mom taught her children about how much God loved them. One of Julie's earliest memories was of her mother kneeling beside her, teaching her to pray. At those prayer times each night, Julie learned to ask Jesus to teach her daddy to love Him too.

Every Sunday morning in their small two-bedroom farmhouse Helen Fehr lined Julie up on the couch with her older siblings, Florence and Ken, to teach them Bible stories and songs. Then they listened together to a Christian radio broadcast.

One Sunday the radio pastor offered a Bible to anyone who would write in and ask for one. Julie wanted a Bible of her own.

"Can we write to 'our' pastor and get one?" she asked her mom.

The Fehr's money was carefully budgeted and there wasn't usually a lot left over. So, in response to Julie's pleading, Helen wrote a letter and sent in some of her precious egg-sale money as a gift to the radio work. And so it was that Julie received her first Bible.

The Fehr family moved to another farm a few miles away, bringing them close to a small church where they attended. The services were in German, but with time Julie could understand what was being said. And Sunday school became the social highlight of her week.

One week the pastor announced a special evangelistic service. Julie went with anticipation. She knew there was going to be lots of singing and special music and many of her friends would also be there. Because it was a special service, Julie listened more carefully than usual to the speaker who explained the story of salvation and then invited people to come to the front of the church if they wanted to ask Jesus to be their Savior.

With heart racing, she began to stand up to go forward, but her friend Ruthie touched her arm and whispered, "This is for people who understand what they're doing. It's not for kids." Disappointed, Julie sat back on the bench, wishing she was older.

It was several months later when the four girls sat together at lunch hour watching the ice melt from the hockey rink. Ruthie, having been corrected, now understood that kids could receive the Lord too. Julie knew that she hadn't always been obedient and she felt naughty about having done things that weren't right. She also knew that her sister Florence had already made a decision to ask Jesus into her heart, and she certainly didn't want Florence to go to heaven without her! This time when Ruthie asked her if she wanted to ask Jesus to come into her heart, Julie's mind was already made up. "Yes, I do."

The girls knelt together on the skate-scarred floorboards of that dressing room. The cuts in the wood hurt Julie's knees, but that didn't matter—she knew she wanted Jesus to live in her heart. The yellow-breasted prairie meadowlarks joined with the angel chorus that day when Jesus Christ took up residence in Julie's heart.

After supper that evening while John Fehr listened to the world news, Julie crawled up on his lap to comb his hair. It was their evening custom, spending some special time together before she went to bed. When the news was over, Julie continued working on her father's hairstyle, but instead of her usual carefree chatter, she was silent. She felt shaky inside as she worked up her nerve to ask him a big question.

"Daddy," she began, as she carefully maneuvered the comb and put his hair in place, "Umm . . . I . . . I let Jesus into my heart today. When are you going to do that?"

John didn't answer Julie's question, but listened more intently to the voice on the radio. Though he didn't acknowledge it, the question did not go unnoticed. It was years later that he too commited himself to Christ. But that night, after the children were all in bed, he said to Helen, "Our Julie—she's going to be a missionary someday."

Julie's teen years were tough. Spiritually speaking, her recollections of them were a "blank." She attended high school in Abbotsford, British Columbia, where her family had moved when she was 10. She never denied being a Christian, but she was rather indifferent about it all. She wasn't allowed to join in many of the things that her friends were doing. Insecure, unsure about who she was and where she fit in, she felt there was not a lot going for being a Christian.

A group of Christian students met at a noon hour Bible club. They were excited about it and encouraged Julie to attend. While others proudly carried their Bibles to club meetings on top of their school books, Julie bought the smallest New Testament she could get her hands on so it could be easily concealed in her pocket or between the pages of a loose-leaf binder.

Julie didn't often go to Sunday school, but she did have some friends who went and were excited about what they were learning there.

Ruby went to a Nazarene church whose Sunday school had a contest every fall. So for two Sundays each year Julie accompanied Ruby to her Sunday school to help her earn points in the contest. If she had gone for the third Sunday they would have enrolled her, and that would never do!

Agnes went to an Alliance church whose Sunday school also had an annual contest to increase its attendance. Again, Julie went for two weeks, and on the third would stay home, as she did most of the year. She looked forward to these Sunday school contests and yet was hesitant to make such a thing part of her life each week.

Julie may not have been allowing God to have control of her life, but she was not out of His hands. God had big things in store for this indifferent teenager. But for awhile He would allow her to continue down her own path.

In the 1950s, the University of British Columbia offered a one-year teacher's certificate. There was a teacher shortage in the province, so they sought to remedy the problem by getting young teachers into the schools after only one year on campus, with encouragement to attend summer sessions for several years to follow.

Now that, thought Julie, *is a pretty quick way to get into the money.* She was already considering a teaching career, but now the decision was sealed.

With certificates in hand, Julie and her friend Selma investigated some possibilities of where they might like to work. Because there were teaching vacancies all over the province, the choices were almost limitless.

Savona, a small town near Kamloops, in British Columbia's arid interior, caught their attention. It was in logging and ranching country and sounded like an adventuresome place to begin their teaching careers. An added bonus was that it was close enough to home that they could get there within a few hours but far enough away that they would not be too closely supervised.

Julie and Selma shared a small teacherage near the shores of Kamloops Lake. They spent their Saturdays on the beach but it didn't feel right to either of them to be at the beach Sunday morning. Their consciences wouldn't permit it. It was not long after they moved to Savona that they took the bus into Kamloops one Friday after school and booked a hotel for the weekend.

After purchasing a copy of the local newspaper, they went straight to the "Come to Church" section. They saw an ad for The Christian and Missionary Alliance church, which Julie remembered was one of the ones her mom had approved of her attending. The decision was made. The Alliance church it would be.

Two nervous young teachers walked up the steps of Kamloops Alliance Church, a small old building with long windows. They'd come this far—there was no turning back now. Their fears were soon put to rest as they were warmly welcomed and even invited to share a meal around the table of one of the church families after the service. Such warmth and exuberance from several families in the church drew them back Sunday after Sunday.

When some folks in the Kamloops church found out that Julie and Selma were staying in a hotel each weekend they wouldn't hear of it. That was certainly not necessary when there were empty bedrooms in so many of their homes. The gals exchanged a hesitant glance. Staying with church families would cramp their Saturday evening plans! But it really did make more sense, so they gratefully accepted the hospitality.

Friday evenings were filled with varied and fun events with the church's lively college and career group, and Saturdays? Well, they were filled with events that Julie and Selma didn't tell anyone much about. But Sunday mornings they were in church before catching the bus back to Savona.

Julie knew that she was living a double life, straddling the fence. It wasn't that she was "wicked, wicked," but neither was she "good, good"! She was trying out both sides, embracing neither. And though she was doing lots of fun things, making good money and dreaming dreams of what she would do with it, deep inside she knew something wasn't right.

It was at Kamloops Alliance that Julie discovered missions—not for herself, of course, but as something that a church did. These people acted as if missions was the reason for the church's existence! They did missions things in Sunday school, they did missions things in the morning worship service and often in the evening service as well. They had special missions rallies any time a missionary was passing through town.

Missionaries are everywhere around here, Julie thought. *This is a bit excessive!*

The missions stories actually became intriguing to her. She didn't take them personally, but they were sure entertaining. What a way to live! These missionaries had a never-ending supply of exciting stories!

Many of Julie's friends in the college and career group felt convicted when missionaries challenged them to invest their lives for God. She sensed their nervousness as they squirmed in their pews, but for Julie there was no conviction. She knew there was no way she could ever be a missionary.

Missionaries inevitably mentioned having to learn at least one foreign language. Julie knew she had a language-learning handicap. She wouldn't qualify. She'd proven it—twice!

French was offered in high school as one way of getting language credits for university studies. It sounded OK, so Julie signed up. However, it wasn't really OK. Try as she might, she just couldn't remember what sound to make when. And if she did remember what sound she was supposed to be making, she couldn't get her tongue and teeth to cooperate in order to make it! And the grammar was no better! The French course did serious damage to her average, so halfway through the first year she dropped it. After all, she didn't expect she would ever find herself in Quebec! Or in France! So why did she need French?

And then came university. Julie was allowed into the teacher's training program on the condition that she pick up a language credit before she could upgrade her certification. She definitely wanted to upgrade since that would translate into higher pay. Thus, it meant a summer of studying German. She had no desire to have another try at French and, since she went to a German-speaking church as a youngster and had memorized some Bible verses in German, she thought it was a wiser choice.

Not long into the summer, Julie's worst fears were realized—German was no better than French! With her marks once again in the danger zone, she went to discuss the situation with her professor. He agreed that the outlook was bleak, but since she had no plans to carry on with German or to take any other courses in his department, he gave her hope that it was possible to squeak through. And that is exactly what she did!

Now in Kamloops Alliance, while her friends fidgeted in their seats, Julie sat smugly knowing that a missionary career was in the realm of the impossible. And yet there was a subtle yearning inside as she realized that being a missionary might be a worthwhile way to invest her life.

During Julie's third year of teaching, Rev. Clarence Shrier came to Kamloops for a week of evangelistic meetings. She and Selma opted to stay in Savona for the week. The last meeting was scheduled for Thursday night. Surely it would be safe to show up for the Friday evening college and career gathering. However, when they arrived at the church, they knew something else was up—more than just college and career people were there.

"What's happening?" Julie asked a friend.

"Have you ever missed a good week!" the answer began. "But you can still get in on it. Rev. Shrier has agreed to stay on for the weekend."

Julie sat through the service that evening feeling miserable inside and wondering why she was even there. *Why didn't we stay in Savona?* she asked herself over and over as the evangelist's words blew past her. But then, some of the words started to sink in and she knew God was speaking to her about being a hypocrite. She felt like a lump of clay trying to mold itself rather than allowing the Potter to do the molding.

When the sermon was over and the invitation came for people to come to the front if they wanted to meet with God, Julie was the first one on her feet and to the altar.

As she tearfully confessed to the Lord the wrong she had done, Rev. Shrier came over and stood by her side. His voice interrupted her praying.

"Julie, is God asking you to be a missionary?"

Lights went on in her head. That is exactly what it was she had been avoiding. She knew then that God was in fact asking her to be a missionary. As she stood at the altar that night she envisioned all her career plans going out the window. But God replaced them with plans of His own all rolled up tight. She couldn't see anything but "overseas" written across the top of the scroll.

Julie's eyes brimmed with tears as she looked heavenward and said, "Yes, Lord, if that's what You want, I'll be a missionary." But she added a condition. "Please, Lord, let me make a difference for Your kingdom. I want it to matter that I have lived."

3

Bad News, Good News

A few weeks later, someone in the Kamloops church asked Julie where she was going to Bible school.

"Bible school?" was her surprised reply.

"Well, yes, of course. If you want to be an Alliance missionary, you'll need to go to Bible school."

Julie hadn't realized that was part of the deal! Where would she go to Bible school? Well, there was no rush to decide since she had to teach for another year to pay off some debts she had accumulated.

There was such an incredible peace in Julie's heart! Things were right between herself and God—she was no longer trying to live with her feet on two different paths. Now she was walking with both feet on God's path. There was a new joy and excitement in reading and studying her Bible as she prepared each week for the Sunday school class she taught. God was so real to her. Her desire was to obey and serve Him.

No longer did the missions emphasis at Kamloops Alliance seem excessive! Julie couldn't get enough. She read every missionary biography she could get her hands on. If she was going to be a missionary, she needed to find out all she could!

The next missionary to come through Kamloops was Mrs. R.G. Burnette who worked in the jungles of Ecuador. She talked about the Jivaro (HE-va-row) headhunters and how she and her husband would soon be retiring from their work among them. Something stirred in Julie's heart. She knew who one of the Burnettes' replacements would be! From then on, the Jivaro people were *her* people!

Julie noticed yearbooks from Canadian Bible College (CBC) lying around on coffee tables in her weekend homes. She hadn't known the Alliance had its own Bible college. She needed to find out more.

To make sure she made the right decision, Julie wrote for information from a few other Bible schools as well. But she discovered CBC was the only one that offered an entire program in missions. Feeling she needed all the help she could get, CBC became the obvious choice.

In the fall of 1960, Julie moved to the windswept prairie city of Regina, Saskatchewan to begin her studies at CBC. She felt nervous about going alone to a city and college where she knew no one. But she told herself, *If you're going to South America, you're going to be on your own, so consider this part of your training.* And so she went.

Julie had something on her mind she couldn't get rid of—language study! Since the night she went forward in the Kamloops church, she knew she was going to have to learn a foreign language. Plagued by her past failures, she felt she needed to prove to herself that she could do it. CBC offered only one foreign language—Greek. Julie enrolled in Greek.

Learning the Greek alphabet and a few simple words wasn't too bad. But that was followed by grammar and sentence structure and an ever-increasing mountain of vocabulary. It felt like French and German all over again. Then came the midterm exam.

Like everyone else in the class, Julie walked around with her vocabulary cards, spending every spare moment trying to squeeze a few more Greek words into her head. She was going through the right motions, but not getting the same results!

Desperate, she paid a visit to Professor Christine Kincheloe's office. Mrs. Kincheloe took out her folder of student grades. "Yes, this is quite serious, isn't it? We do have a problem here," she said staring at Julie from the other side of the desk. "You're not planning to go on to second year Greek, are you?"

"No, no. I'm definitely not planning on that."

"And you're not going to be a Bible translator, are you?"

"Oh my, no! I want to work with people, not with paper. I know I won't be a Bible translator!"

Mrs. Kincheloe was very understanding. Taking into consideration Julie's convictions, effort and strong motivation, she agreed that if Julie stuck it out until the end of the year and kept working the way she was, there was a good chance she would receive credit for the course.

Julie did receive credit for her year of Greek—under the condition that she never try to use it! But that didn't change the way she felt about herself. She'd proven again that she couldn't do it. And yet she knew that God had called her to be a missionary.

Not allowing her experience with Greek to stop her, Julie kept plugging along on her journey to South America. She led the South America prayer group and learned everything she could about the Jivaro people of Ecuador.

Among the many friendships Julie made in Bible college was a special one with a young man. In those days CBC had a rule preventing students from becoming engaged during the school year. That rule stood between the young couple and a promise of marriage. Though they often spoke of spending their future together, all was not well. Julie cared for him deeply, but he was questioning whether or not he was really called to missions. He certainly didn't share her passion for South America.

Maybe Julie wouldn't go overseas after all. Surely God couldn't be asking her to give up the man she loved. The cost was too high. As the weeks passed, she felt convicted about her rebellion. The certainty of her call persisted. She knew she could no longer pursue the relationship.

As a qualified missionary candidate, Julie filled out the necessary forms to apply for overseas service. It was then that she found out she would not be sent to the Jivaro. Only couples were sent to that tribe. What a disappointment! But surely there were plenty of other opportunities in Ecuador.

Then came a tentative appointment to Peru. Julie put considerable thought and prayer into her decision and agreed that she would be willing to accept the appointment. At least it was on the same continent as Ecuador!

In March of her senior year at CBC, Julie had her final interview with the personnel secretary.

"Are you ready for your final assignment for foreign service?" he asked.

It seemed like a long time before Julie was able to answer. *No, I'm not. I've got another interest,* she thought as she struggled with putting a permanent end to that special friendship.

Of course I am. This is what I've spent the last five years of my life working toward, another voice said. She heard herself say, "Yes, I am."

Following the interview, Julie went back to her dorm room and had a good cry. She knew in her heart that she had made the right decision, but that didn't mean it didn't hurt.

A month before graduation Julie got word from the Alliance that her appointment to Peru had been cancelled. There was no explanation.

Now where am I going? Julie questioned. *Have I complained to God too many times? Is He putting me on the shelf?*

Julie went to her room and closed the door. It was time to get serious with God. Through her tears she poured out her heart to Him. Finally she was able to say, "God, I'll go anywhere. Just send me. I'll do anything if You go with me." And then she added to her prayer that of David Livingstone, "Cut every tie that binds me except those ties that bind me to You."

The next morning on her way to class, Julie paused by the large world map in the hallway. She had passed that map dozens of times before, but her eyes had seen only Ecuador. That morning was different. Her gaze enveloped the whole map, a whole world full of countries. How freeing it was to have told the Lord, "Anywhere!" The excitement welled in her heart as she thought that in a few months time she could be anywhere on that huge map!

In the middle of her last month at CBC, April 1964, Julie received word from Alliance headquarters in New York that she had been assigned to Gabon, Africa. She was to begin language study in France that July, less than three months away. She didn't even know where Gabon was, other than it was a long way from South America! But a deep peace assured her that the appointment was from the Lord. So she wrote her letter of acceptance, dropped it in a mailbox, headed straight for the library and picked up an atlas to find her country.

The two months following Julie's graduation from Canadian Bible College were very full. First there was a tour with the college choir. Julie had the opportunity to share her concern about having to learn French. She asked people to pray for her when they saw the French side of their cereal box in the morning and turned it around to read the English side (all labels in Canada are in both French and English). In France, she noted, there wouldn't be an English side! Many people agreed to partner with her in prayer as she began her missionary career.

Following tour, there were busy weeks at home with her family in Abbotsford. With vaccinations complete, barrels packed full of personal belongings and household items for the next four years and passport in hand, it was time to say goodbye.

The bad news was that in France they speak French! Julie was supposed to do the same. She'd tried it before and wasn't successful. That gave her a mental block that started her off below zero.

The good news was that there's something about having to use a language to survive that helps one to learn it. French didn't come easily, but it did come. Within the first month Julie began to sort out what people were saying. Joining in on the conversation, however, was another story! It was frustrating not to be able to share experiences and ideas, or to contribute to a mealtime conversation around the table at the boarding house where she lived. By the time she figured out how to say what was on her mind, the topic had changed!

One autumn afternoon, as Julie walked in Luxembourg Garden, fallen leaves rustling and crunching underfoot, her heart cried out, *How can I serve You here, Lord? How can You be made known to the others in the boarding house and to my classmates? I cannot speak their language.*

God whispered His answer to Julie's heart. "You cannot speak, but you can live. Serving Me here isn't teaching a Sunday school class, singing in the choir or preaching a message in some well-organized church. It is simply living." Julie had chosen two verses from Romans to guide her life: Romans 12:1-2, which include the instruction to "offer your bodies as living sacrifices." That was what God was calling Julie to do there in Paris—be a living sacrifice.

Finally, the hours of French study were rewarded when Julie passed her final exams. She did it! The Lord actually allowed her to comprehend and retain what she needed to communicate in French. Julie was full of awe and gratitude on July 1, 1965 as she boarded a ship headed down the west coast of Africa to her new home in Gabon.

After two weeks at sea, Julie was glad to stand on solid ground and to give her stomach a chance to stop rolling. And it was not just any ground she was standing on. This was Gabon! This was her country! Fear and excitement mingled together as she was warmly welcomed by missionary colleagues who had come to meet her at the Libreville port.

"You have been assigned to the Tsogo tribe," Don Dirks, the field chairman informed Julie, "and will be living in Guevede (Ge-VED-da) with Clara Lou Stucky." Then he added, "The Getsogo language has got to be the hardest language in this country."

Julie couldn't believe what she had heard. Those words went over and over in her mind: *The Getsogo language has got to be the hardest language in this country . . . the hardest in this country . . . the hardest in this country.* It was like a stuck record that she couldn't turn off, playing over and over as she laid in bed that night. She'd just got French study out of the way and now she had to begin studying the hardest of Gabon's more than 40 tribal languages!

Lord, is this fair? she asked. *Have You forgotten my track record? French was bad enough! Are You allowed to do this?*

Julie knew very well that God was allowed to do what pleased Him. "Does not the potter have the right to make out of the same lump of clay some pottery for noble purposes and some for common use?" she read in Romans (9:21). She knew that God, the Master Potter, had the right to make out of her whatever He chose. And if that meant she had to learn Getsogo, the difficult language of the Tsogo people, she would do it.

4

Words Missionaries Don't Use

Julie's first day in Guevede began when the neighborhood roosters announced the arrival of morning. Their raucous calls continued as Julie pulled herself out of bed and looked out the window.

This is it. I am really here, she told herself. *This is my new home.*

As her eyes adjusted, she could see the tops of the jungle trees silhouetted in the early morning light. The scenes she took in would become familiar, living in this isolated corner of Gabon's rain forest. Goats and sheep lounged on the doorstep. Chickens pecked for worms in the yard. Banana plants rippled their broad leaves in the morning breeze.

The large house that Julie shared with Clara Lou Stucky sat on an immense yard up the hill from the village of Guevede. Clara Lou was a nurse and worked in the dispensary treating the ill who came from Guevede and surrounding villages. Clara Lou already spoke Getsogo, as did a few other missionaries who had previously been assigned to the Tsogo people. The language had been reduced to writing and basic language lessons had been prepared.

Julie jumped into her Getsogo study with both feet, often spending more than the required six hours a day in her lessons. Once again she found herself walking around with vocabulary cards and once again she struggled to retain their contents.

Not only were the language and culture new, but so was everything else! Everywhere Julie turned she came face to face with something she'd never experienced before. Taking the laundry to the riverside laundromat and yielding her room to a passing army of driver ants became routine events. Part of her longed for the familiarity and love of her Abbotsford home, while another part loved the fun and excitement of her new life. There was rarely a dull moment.

Something as simple as baking a birthday cake for Clara Lou was an experience with additional complications. Tiny white bugs smiled up at her from the teaspoon of baking powder.

"I can't let a thing like that stop me," Julie joked as she threw the powder into the flour. "If we do, we'll starve to death out here!" Watching the bugs swim for their lives across the mixing bowl, she was assured that when they were baked they'd be harmless. Plus they were too small to change the flavor!

The bugs Julie and Clara Lou consumed didn't make a very big dent in the insect population of Gabon! The jungle swarmed with tiny biting flies that relentlessly welcomed Julie to Gabon and banqueted on her thick untropicalized blood any time she ventured outside without a protective layer of repellent!

Noah could have saved himself some trouble and let these biting flies drown, Julie lamented as she took a break from her vocabulary cards to scratch her red-spotted leg. She decided to count the bites—94 of them below her knee. No wonder she had a constant urge to scratch!

As she continued to study, Julie soon discovered that she had the ability to mimic what others were saying. So village visits became a daily part of her routine.

One afternoon, she made her way along the path between the houses in Guevede village hoping to find someone willing to give her a Getsogo lesson. It was her first time to the village alone without Clara Lou's helpful interpretations.

A woman came rushing out of her doorway, picked up a clod of dried mud and threw it at her little boy who evidently didn't want to go down to the river to fill the gourds with water. Julie stood watching, quite happy that the clod wasn't aimed at her. When the dirt hit its target and the boy reluctantly picked up the empty gourds, the woman burst into a roar of laughter and a stream of Getsogo.

Julie followed her back to her house. Equipped with only her smile and two sentences of Getsogo, Julie sat down on one of the rocks on the doorstep, indicating her intention to stay around awhile. She'd already put on her smile and now offered her two sentences.

"I have come to get ears for your language," she said rather timidly. "May I just listen to you talk?"

Having settled her part of the deal, Julie pulled out her little notebook and a pen. The hostess picked up the basket she was weaving and after a *buedi* (BWAY-dee, "that's good") started chattering to her husband who came out of a side room. Every once in awhile she paused, repeated a word twice, and, if Julie didn't say it back to her, she let out with a "Madamoiselle" that led Julie to believe she'd better wise up if she expected the woman to talk for her! Julie learned to repeat words until she was rewarded with a *buedi*.

Julie and her new friend were just getting into their "talk and listen" game when a young woman walked by carrying several household items in her arm—a hollowed-out log used for a mortar to grind various leaves into a cookable pulp, several kinds of roots used for food and some peanuts. When the lady of the house explained something about, "Madamoiselle . . . Getsogo," she stopped and unloaded her burden. One by one she named the items, waited for Julie to repeat the word, corrected her pronunciation, cheerfully repeated it three times, allowing time to write it down, then vanished with her armload.

Julie had one page full of words and one head full of sounds when her hostess got out a big, black, well-smoked cooking kettle. Julie nearly laughed, mentally recalling an assortment of comic strips about missionary stew. Perhaps she should leave while the going was good!

For fear of out-staying her welcome, Julie expressed her thanks, repeated the goodbyes she'd been taught and started for home. As she made her way up the hill through the red dust of the road and the moist undergrowth of the jungle fringe, she felt like she should be wearing a white pith helmet just to make the picture complete.

Village visits became a part of Julie's daily routine. First, she visited the kitchens of the Christian women who lived near the church. She usually went late in the afternoon when she knew they would be back from spending the day in their plantations (gardens cut out of the forest) and would be chatting with their neighbors while they sliced leaves and scraped taro in preparation for the evening meal.

One afternoon, Julie heard laughing coming from around the fire of one of the "outdoor" kitchens (a small shack set apart from the rest of the house) and joined the Christian women there. Armed with her ever-present notebook, she sat down on a little bench the way she'd been told to do. But nobody said anything, and in a few minutes the women got up, walked away and recongregated at another kitchen.

Julie walked over to the new meeting place. Again silence reigned shortly after she joined them. *What is going on?* Julie wondered. *Are they talking about something they don't want me to hear? Or do they just not want me around? They know I'm trying to learn their language. Why are they so unwilling to help?*

With panic gripping her heart, Julie kept moving through the village. She simply had to find someone who would talk to her. *If the Christian women won't talk to me, I'll find the pagan women,* she decided.

Julie went to the kitchens further away where the pagan women were. And there she was welcomed. Not only did they allow her to be there, but they encouraged her with her language learning. They made her repeat words until she said them correctly and wrote them down. And they laughed together when she made mistakes although Julie often didn't understand just what it was she was laughing at! As long as she brought her notebook, which was like her passport to their kitchens, the pagan women were happy to invite her in and provide her with Getsogo lessons.

A few years later, Pastor Joel and the elders from the Guevede church came to Julie with an apology. They explained that Julie was the fifth missionary to be appointed to the Tsogo people. With the exception of Clara Lou, all the others had been reassigned elsewhere. The people had asked themselves, "What is it? Why do they leave us?"

After some discussion, they decided that as soon as the missionaries learned the language, they left. Therefore, they said, the next time a missionary was sent to them, they wouldn't be so generous in sharing their language. If the missionaries didn't get the language, they wouldn't move away.

Julie was the next missionary! So that was why the Christian women had not welcomed her! What the Tsogo didn't understand is The Christian and Missionary Alliance policy that if a new missionary is not successful at learning a language in two years, they are sent back home.

The pagan women were not in on the scheme to keep Julie around. She felt privileged that she was welcomed, but she also felt a weight of responsibility. More than once, as fetishes hung overhead, she was struck with the possibility that through her friendship and visits, these people could open their hearts to the light of Jesus.

Julie's visits provided all sorts of new words. Looking in the Getsogo dictionary compiled by previous missionaries, she found she was learning many words they hadn't recorded. And then she found out why. When the heart is unregenerate, so is the mouth. Her "enriched" vocabulary included words that missionaries wouldn't normally use!

The day-to-day activities of life in the jungle were much more time-consuming than back home in Canada. And there was constant maintenance.

The Guevede Mission house had running water—most of the time! The system consisted of seven 45-gallon barrels placed under the eaves of the house where the tropical rains kept them filled most of the year. While they collected water, they also collected leaves, insects and rodents. And they also rusted.

The barrels were overdue for a cleaning, but Julie put it off, fearing the process would dislocate some rust flakes and expose holes in the metal. However, the more she thought about the accumulation of rotted leaves, rust and insect bodies, the more convinced she was that she had to take the risk.

The yardman dumped out the water, cleaned the sludge from the bottom of each barrel and dried them out, ready to be refilled by the afternoon rain. Time for the test. He poured some water into each barrel. To Julie's relief, only one of the barrels leaked.

Her solution was to start chewing gum—Wrigley's Doublemint®, received in a package from home. She chewed until all the sugar was out of it. *Better for me to enjoy the sweetness than to have it decompose and turn the water into wine!*

she mused. With the well-chewed gum plastered on the inside of the hole, she applied a patch of solder on the outside. The patch held!

The barrel next to it also sprung a leak. More gum, more solder, and the water system was once again in working order. And it was none too soon. Julie could hear the rain coming. She knew it would be upon them in minutes. Like a locomotive it came, moving across the hills, pulling a white curtain of falling water behind it, drumming down on acres of forest leaves, punctuated by claps and rumbles of thunder. All seven clean water barrels were full in less than an hour!

With the passing of time, Julie understood more and more of the conversations she heard and was able to put together some Getsogo sentences. The village visits became the highlight of her day. During one such visit, some women asked her if she had another name besides "Mademoiselle Sair" (the Getsogo pronunciation of Fehr). When she told them her name was "Julianna" they decided it was just too difficult! Getsogo has no *j, l, f, h, or r*, so there wasn't a lot they could pronounce in "~~J~~u~~l~~ie ~~F~~e~~hr~~"!

Language study involves more than just learning words and sentence structures. Along with the words come the lessons in culture. To celebrate her six-month anniversary in Gabon and to learn about the work of the Tsogo women, Julie accompanied three of them on a trip to their plantation deep in the forest. Having passed her first series of Getsogo exams, she felt ready to try out her vocabulary in the forest where she'd have no word cards to refer to.

She arrived at her friend's house that morning with her thermos of water, her lunch and her precious little green notebook, without which they probably wouldn't have even let her come along. These items were promptly put into a *gésambi* [gay-SAHM-bee, carrying basket) which Julie was to carry. After all, no woman has any business going into the forest without her basket on her back to bring back food and firewood.

The four women and two children caused quite a stir as they passed the last few village homes and disappeared into the forest. People couldn't get over that Madamoiselle was going to go to the plantations! How could anyone *want* to do such a thing?

"Are you going to work too?" Julie was asked.

"No. I haven't got a machete."

"What will you bring back in your *gésambi*?"

"I don't know. Can I go to the forest without it?"

"Oh, no, you must carry it anyway."

Julie followed the others single file down the muddy trail to the plantation, a 30-minute walk from the village. During their four hours there, Julie baby-sat in the shade of huge overlapping taro leaves while the other women cut weeds.

One of them cut eight cobs of corn which she put in the bottom of Julie's *gésambi*. She also showed her how to weed a peanut field and suggested that next time Julie could help her weed and she'd pay her with peanuts. *Talk about "working for peanuts,"* Julie thought.

The group's re-entry at the village caused an even greater stir than their departure. Ears of corn waved their greenery from the top of Julie's *gésambi*, convincing their welcomers that she'd actually been to the plantation. Apparently white women were not expected to "work." When she waved her little green word book at the villagers, telling them she found names for their trees, they were convinced the trip had been worthwhile.

I think I like my "behind the desk" language job better, Julie smiled as she headed up the hill to the Mission station.

5

A One-Person Bed

Something that troubled Julie deeply in those early months in Gabon was her identity. It seemed to her that she had no value. Clara Lou Stucky was a nurse. The villagers called her "nurse." But they didn't know what to call Julie. She was "the missionary who wasn't a nurse." Neither did she understand the culture, nor speak the language. She heard villagers talk to their dogs in Getsogo—the dogs responded. But if someone spoke to her, she couldn't respond; she didn't understand what people were saying. She saw her value as less than that of a dog. Her self-worth was about as low as it could get. What was she even there for?

Having had experience teaching children in Canada, Julie hoped that she would be able to establish relationships with Gabonese children. But, to her dismay, they were terrified of her white skin and scattered when she walked by. "The white one, the white one!" they cried in terror. The bravest among them slowly and uncertainly approached her and ran their fingers over her arm. Or if they couldn't reach that high, they slid their hands down her leg, unable to believe that such white skin could actually have substance to it.

And then she found out why the youngsters were so afraid of her. Among the Tsogo, white people were the equivalent of the North American "boogey-man." Mischievous young Tsogos were warned to "be good or the white woman will come and throw you into the fire." Or, "look out or the white woman will eat you." Was it any wonder they ran in terror when Julie entered their homes? It didn't take her long to realize that she wouldn't be having a ministry among the children very soon.

Learning something of the role and value of women in Tsogo culture didn't do much for Julie's self-esteem either. A Tsogo woman's identity was based on her association with men. A woman was the daughter of one man, then the wife or concubine of another. That is who she was. Julie didn't fit into any of these categories. She was a single woman. In the minds of the Tsogo, the only women who chose to remain unmarried were prostitutes.

Julie was shocked the day she found out that that was how she was perceived. "The missionary who isn't a nurse" was too long a title for the villagers to use all the time, so they merely shortened it to "Mademoiselle," the French term for "Miss." One day, after hearing the title "Mademoiselle" countless times, Julie came home and mentioned their obsession with titles to Clara Lou.

Clara Lou had been in Gabon for 12 years and understood the meaning of "Mademoiselle." Because a single woman didn't belong to one man in particular, it only made sense that she was available for any man!

Julie felt sick inside. Her mind reeled with questions. *How can they possibly think that I am a prostitute? How can I ever have a ministry among these people? How will they ever learn about a holy God if they think that the one telling about Him is a prostitute? How can I even sit in their kitchens and listen to them speak when they greet me, "Hi, Prostitute. Come and sit by my fire, Prostitute"?*

Crying out to God in her loneliness and bewilderment, she began to doubt that He had really called her to Gabon. The assurance that got her through Bible college and enabled her to end the special friendship seemed to vanish. She thought of Jesus' first 12 disciples and noted that they were all men. *When did God start calling women?* she asked herself. *Perhaps this was my own idea to do the heroic thing and travel across the globe for some fun and adventure under the guise of being called by God.*

The loneliness in Julie's heart was intense—a constant, haunting emptiness compounded by her new-found knowledge that those to whom she came to minister saw her as a prostitute. She cried herself to sleep at night, telling God again and again that she wanted to go home. She confessed to Him that she had made a mistake in coming to Gabon in the first place.

I was never meant to be a missionary, she told Him. *I somehow got it all wrong in thinking I was. I'm sorry. You know I don't have the money for a ticket home. Please send it to me. I'll go home and apologize to the churches and tell them I was all wrong. It's all my fault. Just send the money.*

Mail service to Guevede was not very regular so Julie knew it would be a while before the money for her flight home arrived. While she waited for it, she carried on with her language study, pretending she was going to be a missionary. After all, that was what she was being paid to do!

One afternoon while memorizing Getsogo vocabulary, Julie slowly poured kerosene through an old felt hat to filter out the debris. Her eyes left what she was doing and went to the world map hanging on the wall. Ecuador, where she had been so sure God had called her to work, sat on the equator. Her eyes followed that line east across South America and the Atlantic Ocean and came to rest on Gabon, also on the equator. She located where she thought the unmarked Guevede Mission station might be—about as close to the equator as one could wish for.

She forgot about her vocabulary as she continued to draw comparisons between Ecuador and Gabon. In addition to lying on the equator, both countries were on the west coast of their continents, they were similar in size and both were covered with tropical rain forests. Then she recalled some of what she had studied about the Jivaro headhunters, the cannibalistic Ecuadorian tribe. There were many similarities between them and the formerly cannibalistic Tsogo tribe.

But there was nothing in North American libraries written about the Tsogo. There was no way Julie could have studied them. The best way she could have prepared to work among the Tsogo would have been to study the Jivaro. And that is exactly what God had her do!

That thought was a gentle reminder to Julie that she was precisely where God wanted her to be. Somehow she knew that the money for the flight home wouldn't come. She was still struggling with the language and was desperately lonely, but she was beginning to learn that God was sufficient for her in whatever situation she would find herself—including being thought of as a prostitute!

Several months later Clara Lou, whose health was failing, made a trip to Schweitzer's Hospital, nearly 400 kilometers (264 miles) away. She offered to drop Julie off at one of the villages not far from Guevede and pick her up on the return trip. It sounded like a good opportunity to practice her Getsogo and, though she'd never stayed overnight alone in one of the villages before, Julie had visited this one and knew some of its people. She gladly accepted the offer.

After unloading Julie's three boxes of luggage, Clara Lou continued on her way. Julie tried to ignore the fear in her heart as she heard the sound of the four-wheel drive fade into the jungle. The chief and others came to welcome her to their village. Hospitality is very important among the Tsogo—they were going to take good care of this visiting "white child."

The chief and his wife vacated their house so Julie would have a place to stay. Faces filled the doorway and windows as she began to unpack her belongings from their well-padded, dust-proof, insect-proof and moisture-proof tin boxes. It was awkward—awkward for her and awkward for them.

As she slowly set up her table and camp stove and hung her mosquito net with many pairs of eyes following each move, she was aware of a conversation going on between the chief and a village elder. Since no Gabonese woman would be permitted to travel without her husband or children, Julie knew they were talking about her being alone and was pretty sure there was talk about her needing male company for the night.

She interrupted their conversation, assuring the men that, although it appeared she was alone, she really wasn't. God was with her. From the blank looks on their faces Julie knew she wasn't getting through.

With her heart racing, she resumed her unpacking, hoping that the novelty of watching her set up her camp cot would deflect the conversation. As she slid the poles of the cot into place, she heard shouting out in the courtyard. The same phrase was repeated several times before Julie caught what they were saying.

"It's a one-person bed! It's a one-person bed! She brought her own bed and it's only wide enough for one person!" Julie chuckled with relief. The size of her bed had convinced them she was serious when she said she intended to spend the night alone!

That night, as Julie lay in her one-person bed listening to the peaceful buzz of the jungle night, she thanked God that He was beginning to solve the problem of her image—without her help! She was learning anew that He was sufficient for all her needs and that her identity was in her relationship with Him, not in whether or not she was married. She was God's woman, and that was what mattered.

6

A Serious Question

Within the brackets of sunrise and sunset each day, Julie remained in persistent pursuit of new words. She continued to make progress with much encouragement from her village audience.

"You *will* learn, you *will* hear, you *will* speak," they told her with never-ending optimism. And Julie enjoyed it more and more.

The last phase consisted of gathering Tsogo legends, parables and proverbs, a refreshing change from the first year and a half of memorizing words and trying to grind them out in the right order. Julie loved to sit with the little old ladies whose stories were frequently interrupted by a puff on a pipe or the correction of a child playing nearby. And she never tired of listening to the old men throw out their parables and legends for her tape recorder to catch, egging each other on with grunts, clicking of their tongues and sounds of exclamation.

At long last, in June of 1967, Julie passed her final Tsogo exams and moved out of the compartment labeled "Language Student," into the one labeled "Senior Missionary." What a joy to feel like she could now get on with being a *real* missionary!

With formal language study behind her, Julie had much more time to devote to teaching and evangelism. Pastor Joel of the Guevede church organized a two-week evangelism trip to several Tsogo villages which were without pastors. Julie was invited to be part of the team.

To ensure that the roads in the Tsogo mountains would be passable, the trip was scheduled for the dry season. But that didn't mean the roads were good! Speed averaged 12 miles an hour driving in and out of gullies, ridges and ravines that crisscrossed the mountain road. To Julie it looked like "a stairway gone wild!"

Each team member went prepared to preach, lead singing or pray at any given stop. When they arrived in Nombo, Pastor Joel told Julie, "Tonight you will teach here."

The small thatch-roofed chapel was crowded with black faces. A low-flamed kerosene lantern hung above the pulpit so Julie could read her notes. But she couldn't see any faces—only the sparkling eyes and white teeth of the believers who had gathered for the service. The cicadas in the roof were whistling back and forth to each other as she began to tell the story of the prodigal son, using the question and answer style she had been taught.

The first time she asked a question there was a response. Incredible! She was actually communicating! She threw out another question. Again the little chapel came alive as answers were given. This was exhilarating! Those two years of studying seven or eight hours a day were paying off. It worked! She was teaching in Getsogo and being understood!

Julie worked her way through her message, emphasizing each point with her ever-expressive hands, and the response continued. She later found out that she had made the prodigal son a lot more prodigal than he really was because of the vocabulary she had collected visiting in those pagan kitchens! No wonder there was such a lively response that night in the Nombo chapel!

The next morning the village chief (who was not a Christian) along with Pastor Joel and other members of the evangelism team told Julie they wanted to talk to her.

"We have never heard a missionary use our language the way you do," Pastor Joel encouraged.

Wow! thought Julie. *What a compliment!* She waited for him to continue.

"God gave you our language." The tone of Joel's voice was serious. "When God gives a gift to any of His children it's not for that child alone. It's for the whole Church—for His body.

He's given you Getsogo and it's so that we can have the New Testament in our language."

Julie's mind was racing. *Just a minute, here,* she thought. *Gave? How can they say God* gave *me Getsogo? What about the two years of studying? What about the extra time I put in above what was required?* Gave? *What kind of a gift is that? I* earned *it!*

Unable to find the words she was looking for, Julie began to rattle off her reaction.

"No, I'm not a translator. Bible translators are trained—they're specialists. I haven't had that training. Plus missionaries have to be assigned to translation. They don't just decide to do it."

On and on she went while the group listened patiently. When she concluded, they answered, "We don't understand how decisions are made in your country, but we know that God has sent you to us so that we can have the New Testament in our language."

Julie's thoughts flashed to her Greek studying days at Canadian Bible College. She as much as promised her professor that she wouldn't be a translator. She thought of how she loved to spend time in the villages with the people and that she didn't like paper work. There was no way she could be a translator.

She opened her mouth to reiterate her protest.

"Don't give us your answer now," Pastor Joel said. "You're going to your country soon. We'll give you until you come back from there to tell us."

Julie had learned that in Tsogo country you could judge the importance of a question by how long someone was willing to wait for an answer. If it was a simple everyday issue, the answer was expected within an hour. If it was something that really mattered, they'd give you a whole week. But they gave Julie over a year! This was serious!

"There's just one thing we ask you to do while you're gone," Pastor Joel added. "When you go to your country, pray each day and ask God, 'Do you really want the Tsogo people to have the New Testament in their own language?' "

While Julie was on her first furlough back in Abbotsford, she didn't pray that prayer. She couldn't. That wasn't the kind of work she wanted to get into. But she couldn't forget Pastor Joel's question. Nor could she forget the people telling her that God had *given* her their language.

Then one day it was like God tapped her on the shoulder. "Julie, remember how you did at language learning in the past," He said. "I *did* give you Getsogo. I gave you the endurance and the capacity to mimic and retain. I did it. They're right. I *gave* you their language."

Julie couldn't fight that—she knew God was right. The months went by and with the passing of time Julie had a growing assurance that God did in fact want her to be a translator.

Once more He had reminded her that a life given to Him could be molded into whatever vessel He saw fit. And He was molding her into a Bible translator.

By the time furlough was over, Julie was beginning to get excited. *What if the Tsogo had the New Testament because I had lived among them?* she asked herself. That was something to get excited about—something that would truly make a difference in the kingdom of God.

7

Monyepi

Enoch and his wife Esther were thrilled to hear Julie say that her understanding of Getsogo was, in fact, a gift from God, and that she was committed to the translation of the New Testament into their language. Enoch was a Tsogo Bible teacher from the village of Nombo where Julie had told the story of the prodigal son more than a year earlier.

The task ahead was overwhelming! Deciding it would be wise to start with smaller, more manageable projects, Julie began work on the translation and revision of a Getsogo hymnbook and some selected verses and chapters of Scripture used in Bible studies. She also spent hours transcribing native stories from tape to paper, pouring over them in search of word meanings and sentence structures. She wanted to learn the Tsogo style of narration in which to write the narrative sections of the Gospels and Acts.

The International Bible Society at that time had an office in Cameroon, Gabon's neighbor to the north. Julie contacted them and she and Pastor Joel were invited to attend a month-long translator's institute.

Armed with her new-found knowledge and enthusiasm, yet still feeling like she was in over her head, Julie started seriously into Scripture translation.

One thing that became apparent early in her work was that it was not wise to rely on the people of Guevede for corrections. Missionaries had been in Guevede for many years and the people were used to the errors made in their language. They were too permissive and would allow errors to continue rather than correct each one. If they understood what was being said (or written), that was good enough.

Julie talked this problem over with Enoch and Esther who were becoming her village Mama and Papa. Enoch had a locale in mind. It was a village he wanted to visit and, if Julie accompanied him, they could combine teaching with translation.

A trip was planned. Julie would have supper in Nombo with Enoch and Esther and spend the night. The next day they would travel.

Supper that day was a memorable one. Julie and Mama Esther were talking and waiting for the men to come in from the forest when Papa Enoch arrived with a squirming package about the size of a football wrapped up in leaves.

"Do you know what these are?" Esther asked as she opened a little slit in the package.

Gulp! Julie did know. They were *tsombes* (TSOHM-bees), the larvae of the big black rhinoceros beetle, residents of the uppermost section of a palm tree. As a reward for her correct identification of the creatures, Julie was told she could have some of them!

How can I turn down such a magnanimous gesture? Julie thought. *John the Baptist, move over with your locusts. Here I come with my* tsombes!

The larvae were about two inches long and as round as an adult thumb, fatter in the middle and tapered at each end, covered in soft skin and a hairy fuzz. When cooked, the fuzz would all lie down nice and flat!

Julie suffered no ill effects after her feast of *tsombes*, but given the choice between a hamburger on a bun and five *tsombes* on a bun there was no competition. She consoled herself with the thought that John the Baptist probably didn't learn to eat locusts in a single day either!

The next morning the teaching/translation team set out for the "City-of-Bridges." That was Julie's nickname for a cluster of village suburbs that ambled along both sides of the main road and across the river. It was not a city and it had nothing that anyone in North America would call a bridge. But it did have two log contraptions that did the job.

The one they crossed was high in the air above the swirling current. It was a haphazard arrangement of logs, each a different size, shape and length, and all in various stages of disintegration. They were held together by faith and vines—mostly faith! Each time Julie lifted a foot, at least one log would change its mind about where its position in life should be! The redeeming feature was a vine that resembled a handrail. It was very slack and ineffective, but at least it gave some feeling of security should one's feet slip.

Safely on the other side, Julie and the others saw a thick old military coat standing in the courtyard. The coat moved to greet them. A little old man, like a twig lost in mossy wrappings, reached out to shake their hands and welcome them to his suburb. His name, translated into English, was Tobacco.

Tobacco had heard the Word of God taught before and he wanted to hear more. He called the people of the village together.

"Come and hear the truth," he invited. "The matters these people teach are truth."

Papa Enoch had asked Julie to teach. The lesson was on Christ's resurrection, a story they had never heard before. The crowd was with her all the way, indignant over the treatment Jesus received. They leaned forward in their chairs as she told of Christ's body being laid in the tomb. Then when they heard of Mary coming in the morning, finding the stone rolled away and thinking the body had been stolen, they all agreed and nodded. No doubt about it—the corpse had been stolen. Julie could imagine their minds clicking as they thought about the value of such a corpse and all the potent fetishes that could be prepared from it, since Jesus had powers of healing and prophecy.

Curious to find out who had stolen the body, Julie's audience gave her their full attention. She told of the angel asking Mary why she was looking for the living among the dead. The villagers looked at one another with questioning looks. That didn't make sense.

Julie went on, telling of Mary's discovery that Jesus had in fact risen. She was interrupted by exclamations of amazement.

"Can you believe that?" came from one.

"A dead one came alive again!" said another.

Julie told them that the Christ she was teaching about is still alive and that He is the only way to walk on God's path. As she concluded, Tobacco nodded and said, "We like that."

After the service the villagers scattered, leaving Julie and Enoch to talk with Tobacco and his nephew Mandoh, the village chief. Julie told them about her search for Getsogo words.

"Will you help me find the right words to say what God has to tell you?" she asked them. She showed the men the mimeographed pages of the Gospel of John and explained that was only a small part of God's message. She told them that though she knew a lot of Getsogo words, she wasn't always able to write them the way a

Tsogo reader would immediately understand. Would they help her find more words so more of God's message could be in their own language?

Tobacco had no problem believing that the markings on the paper "leaves" were a message from God. The Tsogo tribe had long believed that God wrote a message to people. It was in the form of strange markings made on leaves found in the jungle. The markings are made by insects who eat the chlorophyll as they work their way across the leaf, leaving a mysterious trail in their wake.

The Tsogo knew that the markings were made by an insect, but believed a Creator God sent the insect to give them this message in written form. The problem was in deciphering that message! Even the village elders full of years and full of wisdom could not interpret those "writings of God" as the leaf messages were called. So when Julie opened the Gospel of John and told the villagers, "These are the writings of God," no one doubted that the whole collection of "leaves" was God's message to all people.

Tobacco looked at the pages in Julie's hand.

"When I look at those papers," he told her, "I see the markings of a chicken who walked in mud. When you look at them, you say, 'God has said. . . .' We want more of these words in our village. We will help you to find them."

Tobacco continued.

"A child needs to be told again and again, day after day, not to touch a sharp knife," he explained. "Finally it will understand and turn away from the knife to something else. That's the way it is with us. That's what we need. You have told us once, but we still don't know. You have to be here often and tell us again and again. Then we will know the truth."

Crossing back over the log bridge, Julie's heart bubbled with emotion. It was exciting to have been welcomed so warmly, to see the hunger for truth in Tobacco and to have help with translation. Yet there was also sadness. Yes, they would be back to teach, but it couldn't be every day, nor every week. And so the residents of the City-of-Bridges remained in darkness.

Several weeks later, Julie and Enoch were once again on their way to the City-of-Bridges when they stopped to offer a ride to an elderly couple walking along the road. It was Tobacco and his wife.

"What is your name?" Tobacco's wife asked Julie.

"Sair," Enoch answered for her, using the Tsogo pronunciation of Fehr.

"But don't you have a *real* name?" the woman persisted.

Julie didn't know how to respond. "Sair" was a real name as far as she was concerned! She paused and looked at the woman questioningly.

"Well," Tobacco's wife continued, "know that your name is *Monyepi* (mohn-YEP-ee). I've named you Monyepi."

Enoch asked if she accepted the name. Julie replied affirmatively, although at the time she couldn't remember what it meant!

Others came out of their houses to greet the visitors and Tobacco's wife introduced Julie as Monyepi.

"Ah yes," said an elderly man. "That is a good name. Look at her." As he spoke he moved his hands through the air outlining an hourglass figure.

Horrors! thought Julie. *Is that what my new name means?*

There was a nodding of heads and a general agreement that Julie's name was right for her. Tobacco nodded his approval.

"It is a good name for you," he said. "My wife and I had a long walk home with our baskets, but you made the trip beautiful for us."

Yes, that's it! Julie thought, remembering the meaning of the root word *nyepa* (n-YEP-a). She was pleased that she had accepted the name. Who wouldn't want to be Monyepi, which means "beautiful one" or "lovely one"?

Tobacco's wife made sure the villagers who came to meet them knew that Julie now had a *real* name. They all tried it out, agreeing that it was a good name for her. Then Tobacco spoke up again in the hearing of all who were gathered.

"Monyepi, that's you," he said, beginning another explanation of her name. "Because the words you speak and the matters you teach are matters of beauty, loveliness and truth, that is your name. They are words that beautify our lives."

As he did on Julie's previous visit to the City-of-Bridges, Tobacco called together the villagers to hear the teaching about Jesus. Julie had come prepared with picture books to help them remember the lessons she taught, since none of them could read. A picture of a lantern reminded them that Jesus said, "I am the Light of the world," and that those who walk with Him are to be light for other people. A picture of a cross represented the story of Jesus' death and resurrection. With each lesson, different pictures were added to the book, which also served as a reward for faithful attendance.

Tobacco wasn't always sure which "lid" of his book to open, but with practice his old eyes got quite good at "reading" the pictures. It wasn't long until he decided that the path of Jesus was the path he wanted to follow. He declared that he believed Jesus was stronger than the spirits and that Jesus would protect him if he destroyed his fetishes. So, beginning with the dried weasel skin hanging over his doorway, he threw each one of them into a raging fire.

A fetish is a sacred object believed to protect its owner from evil spirits. There is no limit to the number and variety of things that can be fetishes—everyday items such as carvings and bracelets, as well as animal parts and other items more obviously associated with sorcery. Even the remains of a human brain, a highly prized fetish, was kept to bring successful hunting to its owner!

Another cherished possession was the skull of a male ancestor (not that of a female, since only males were believed to have any wisdom), kept in a bark box and consulted for advice.

Fetishes play an important role in the lives of many Tsogo people and they are not easily given up. The people know that the powers of darkness are real and shouldn't be taken lightly. Even believers know fear (or at least apprehension) when they make a break with their old ways and throw their fetishes into the fire. New Christians often entertain lingering doubts as to whether or not they did the right thing and if Jesus really has conquered Satan and his demons.

Though closely attached to their fetishes, their owners are not at peace. Rather, they are locked into a life of fear of displeasing the spirits, breaking a taboo or being cursed by another. Theirs is a constant fear and yet there is a bigger fear of discarding the only system of religion they know.

Many of the pagan rites and rituals practiced throughout Gabon originated with the Tsogo people. This tribe, living deep in the forest, developed a barbaric system of rites and customs.

As they were captured and taken as slaves by other tribes or sold to coastal tribes in exchange for salt and cloth, the captives took their customs with them.

Many of their dances and rites were adapted by other tribes. When certain practices were forbidden by law, the forest-dwelling Tsogo, living far from police and government officials, still clung to their traditional ways. For years after other tribes had become "civilized," the Tsogo carried on with their religious system and were, because of this, looked down upon by other Gabonese.

This was the system of belief into which Julie and Enoch brought the liberating news of Jesus Christ. Tobacco noticed that they did not own any fetishes. This told him it must be possible to live without them. But it was still a very difficult decision for him to make. He had some doubts as he stood beside the fire, watching the smoke and sparks from his fetishes fill the night air. Yet he knew he had made the right decision.

During their stay in the City-of-Bridges, Julie and Enoch took turns teaching the villagers. In between lessons, Julie spent as much time as she could in translation, asking question after question of the villagers, searching for words to enable them to hear God speak in their language.

One afternoon she was looking for a word or phrase to express Paul's "manner of living" or "way of behaving" among the Thessalonians (see 1 Thessalonians 1:5).

One old man spoke up.

"Monyepi," he said, "that's why you got that name. It's all part of the name. It's not only your teaching that makes God's words attractive to the people, but your way of living is one that also beautifies the Word."

Attracted by God's Word and the beautiful character they witnessed in His servant, the inhabitants of the City-of-Bridges were beginning to warm up to the gospel of Jesus Christ.

8

Nyondo

Nyondo (Nee-ON-doh) was on a search for truth. As a child he was full of questions, always asking about the meaning and purpose of life. In his teen years he learned the teachings of his ancestors but was not satisfied with them. So he listened to his uncle who tutored him in the ways of a non-evangelical "white man's religion," which, so his uncle claimed, was superior to the Tsogo teachings.

After repeated drillings of what he had learned, Nyondo was ready for baptism. He was baptized. But he was no different from what he had been before. For all he had learned, there was no change in his heart.

Nyondo spent more and more time with his uncle, wanting to emulate him because of his senior position in this religion. As he watched his uncle and saw him do things that were not becoming for one of his status, Nyondo became disillusioned with what he saw.

"Why do you do these things?" Nyondo questioned.

"It is not for the egg to correct the bird," was his uncle's abrupt reply.

With many unanswered questions on his mind, Nyondo traveled to Nombo to visit relatives. There he spent time with another uncle—Enoch, the Bible teacher. Enoch traveled from village to village with Alliance missionary Austin Parliman. Nyondo accompanied them and listened to them teach. What he saw as they walked together was strikingly different from what he had seen on walks with his other uncle. The lives of these men evidenced that their hearts had been changed by God.

Both Austin and Enoch taught out of a book, the mimeographed copy of the Gospel of John, which had already been translated into Getsogo. Some of the Tsogo villagers had the same book and followed along with the words being read. Nyondo's heart told him, "Here is truth. The white man and my uncle cannot say anything that the other men will not see in their books. I had better get off the path I'm on so I don't become like my other uncle. I'm coming on this path so that I'll be like Uncle Enoch."

Nyondo purchased his own copy of the Gospel of John which Enoch explained to him was only a small part of God's Word to people. His questioning eyes began to study the first Getsogo Scriptures. As the words on the page reached his hungry heart, he knew at last that what he had found was truth.

Months later, Enoch introduced Nyondo to Julie and told him of her project to work on the translation of the entire New Testament. Though Nyondo was very enthusiastic about the prospect of having God's Word in his mother tongue, being involved in the work of translation was the farthest thing from his mind. His plan was to be a nurse and he had enrolled in the nursing school run by Alliance missionaries in Bongolo, 45 kilometers (30 miles) from Guevede.

Not far into his studies, Nyondo encountered problems. He had not studied enough French to cope with the vocabulary used in the nursing text books. Bongolo school had to dismiss him.

Since Nyondo had already uprooted and left his home, Pastor Joel wondered if he would consider moving to Guevede to become Julie's translation assistant. He agreed and, along with his wife Ngonde (Ne-GOHN-da) and their young son, moved into the house next door to Julie on the Guevede hill.

So that he could work with Julie full-time, Nyondo taught his wife how to check his trap lines, a task that is definitely a man's work. They wanted to serve the Lord together, which meant learning new things for both of them. While Ngonde checked their trap lines, Nyondo learned to type. Julie also taught him what she had learned so far about translation and they continued to learn together. Frequently they marveled that God was using them, both untrained ordinary vessels, to bring His Word, His treasure, to the Tsogo tribe.

A tropical storm was brewing as Julie finished typing the verses she and Nyondo had translated that morning. She was ready to blow out her lamp and go to bed when she heard a voice outside her door. It was Nyondo's wife.

"Monyepi, your brother is dying," Ngonde cried. "His body is burning with fever. Come quickly. He is dying." With that she began to wail, crying out in anguish.

Julie grabbed her flashlight and hurriedly accompanied Ngonde across the yard to their house. She found Nyondo, bathed in beads of perspiration, lying on his bed in a coma, his mother wailing beside him. Julie touched his forehead. She was shocked at the heat she felt. Ngonde explained through tears that when she came home from her plantation that afternoon Nyondo was in bed sleeping. She woke him up for supper, but he didn't want to eat. He fell back to sleep and had not wakened since. Ngonde was sure her husband was dying.

Julie gave Nyondo's young son her flashlight and told him to go and get the pastor. But the heat of Nyondo's fever told her they couldn't wait until the pastor arrived before praying. She hushed Nyondo's wife and mother and asked Ngonde to pray first. That would give her time to think. What should she do next?

The only nurse in the area was Anita Reader who had taken Clara Lou's place as Julie's housemate. But she was away. There was no one to turn to for medical help. Prayer was the only tool they had. In her personal Bible study, Julie had been looking into the laying on of hands. Now was the time to put into practice what she was learning.

When Ngonde finished her brief prayer, Julie nervously stretched out her hand and laid it on Nyondo's wet shoulder. She began to pray, not feeling much faith or confidence, but simply asking God to honor His Word and heal His child. Wanting to give God time to do whatever it was He was going to do and hoping to give the pastor time to arrive, she prayed at length.

Into that tense atmosphere peace gradually came. By the time Julie said "Amen," Nyondo's body was completely dry and cool! Moments later Pastor Joel and two of the elders arrived. They anointed Nyondo with red palm oil and Joel led in prayer. He reminded the Lord of all the years the church had craved the Word in their own language. Now that they had a translator, would He please lengthen Nyondo's life and restore his strength? And while He was at it, would He please heal Nyondo quickly so that he wouldn't lose a lot of translation days lying in bed!

To the amazement of all in the room, Nyondo himself began to pray in a loud voice, praising God for restoring him and allowing him to live. He then told the others that when Julie prayed his body responded and he began to feel stronger with each passing moment.

They sang a hymn as other believers arrived to join the prayer and celebration. In the middle of their singing, a powerful storm broke loose. Lightning cracked through the night sky, accompanied by deafening claps of thunder. Wind drove the rain down on the tin roof, making conversation impossible. But the sound of voices raised together in praise could be heard above the tumult.

When the storm subsided around 2:30 a.m., Nyondo was feeling much better, though ready for sleep. Julie walked home under a starry sky, elated with the realization that God had used her obedience to work in Nyondo's body.

That was Saturday night. Monday morning Nyondo was back to work with a story of his own.

He had, he said, left work at noon on Saturday to go check his trap lines. He hadn't gone far into the forest when he suddenly felt dizzy and sick to his stomach. He sat down and leaned against the base of a palm tree, feeling himself about to lose consciousness. He tried to open his eyes, but saw only darkness. His body went limp and he began to perspire.

"Lord, is this where my body will be found?" Nyondo prayed. "Is it today? Is this where I am going to leave the earth? Am I also going to be found at the base of a palm tree?"

Similar things had been happening to other believers. A number of leaders had died, some of them mysteriously. One elder had been murdered, his body found at the base of a palm tree. Nyondo thought his fate was to be the same, that he was falling prey to a curse.

"There's a Tsogo proverb that explains how I felt," Nyondo went on. "It says, 'Lick the honey, you have sweetness, but lose the salt. Lick the salt, you have sweetness, but lose the honey.' "

Julie knew that salt was considered sweet, much as honey is. But she didn't understand what Nyondo meant.

"Explain that to me," she said. "I'm not sure I understand."

"It's as if I had a pool of honey in the palm of my hand," Nyondo replied, "and grains of salt on the back of it. Both are good but I could not have both. I sat under the tree thinking about it. I just wanted to go to be with God. That would be like licking the honey from the palm of my hand while the salt fell to the ground. Then I thought of the salt on the back of my hand. The family of God would suffer fear and more persecution if I died so mysteriously. My wife and children would be left without a provider. And who would finish my translation work? I have not completed the work God gave me to do."

Nyondo looked at the back of his hand. "I struggled. This side salt." Turning his hand over he said, "This side honey. Which should I lick?"

He paused briefly.

"I told God, 'I suppose I must leave the honey for another time. I am not finished here, so I will lick the salt.' "

Gradually strength began to return to him, he said. He slowly stood up and started walking home. He went straight to bed, where he stayed until after Julie and the others prayed for him.

Several weeks later, Julie and Nyondo translated the first chapter of Paul's letter to the Philippians. They got to the 23rd and 24th verses, in which Paul wrote concerning life and death: "I am torn between the two: I desire to depart and be with Christ, which is better by far; but it is more necessary for you that I remain in the body."

"I know what Paul meant," Nyondo smiled, reminding Julie of the day in the forest when he was staring death in the face. "Heaven was so welcoming, but I knew that I had to stay here and finish the work God called me to do." Paul's dilemma was that he wanted to lick the honey and be with Christ, but felt it more necessary to lick the salt and stay with the church. It was a translation that every Tsogo reader would understand, another of the blessings that God brought out of Nyondo's brush with death.

Once again, Julie made a trip to the City-of-Bridges. This time Nyondo and Ngonde went with her and stayed with relatives. Julie stayed in Mandoh's house, where a bedroom had been reserved for her.

"Monyepi, here is some food for you," she heard several times a day as bowls of food were delivered from various sections of the village. Someone had caught a gorilla. Six times in one day the bowls were full of fresh gorilla meat and cooked bananas!

In between their multiple meals, Julie and Nyondo worked on translation. They gathered a committee of villagers to help them decide what words they needed.

"Both words say one thing," one of the men told Julie as they discussed the best way to express a certain idea.

"Is there not a slightly different meaning between the two?" she asked.

"No, Monyepi," he went on. "In Getsogo we have two words for almost each thing. One thing, two words. One thought, two words."

"That's right," the other echoed. "We can use two separate sets of words to say the same thing."

Their revelation confirmed Julie's suspicions and explained those times when she had been following a conversation one minute, and then been completely lost a minute later. It didn't do much to encourage her that she would ever be able to master this complicated language! But it did encourage her that it was a wise thing to talk over each newly translated passage of Scripture with these folks who took the time to answer her questions and work with her to make it right.

On another occasion the committee was discussing the meaning of "new birth," a phrase that had been used in the Guevede church for years. Older villagers questioned how one could have "new birth" that lasted for one's lifetime. Julie found out that the word for "new" means "recent," or "just happened," and does not carry the meaning of "another kind" or "different" as in both English and French. No wonder the Guevede believers had misunderstood the biblical idea of growing and maturing in the Christian life. How could someone be mature and brand new at the same time? They decided instead to use the phrase "the second birth, that of the Spirit."

That was only the beginning of a list of treasured language used in Guevede that the old villagers could not "hear" or understand. Julie and Nyondo found out that the words they'd used for "temptation," "faith," "testimony" and "miracle" had drastically different meanings in everyday village life. The "Christian" Getsogo used in Guevede was not understood outside of the church circle.

Julie and Nyondo worked several hours each day on translation, meeting together with Tobacco and others who aided them in their search for words. One day Nyondo led the group in prayer at the beginning of a meeting. "Lord, You know Getsogo better than we do," he prayed. "So if You were to stand in our church today and say the same things that were written down in Greek, how would You say them? Please show us." Julie's heart warmed within her as he prayed. That was the secret of their translation—to say things the way the biblical Author would have said them if He were using Getsogo.

Not long after that prayer, one old fellow was listening as the committee read one of Paul's letters. Suddenly he spoke up. "That's really our language!" he exclaimed. "I can hear what God is saying." It was moments like that that renewed Julie's commitment to keep going—the Tsogo people were beginning to hear God speak in their own language.

Although working in the City-of-Bridges was helpful, there was one thing that was less than ideal. The villagers' hospitality was so generous that the team experienced constant interruptions. Julie appreciated their kindness and she certainly didn't want to offend them by asking them to leave her alone, but she and Nyondo needed some uninterrupted translation time.

One day Julie had an idea. What if she would ask to live in the City-of-Bridges? She could build a small house in the village where she and Nyondo could work. The villagers would know she wanted to be with them and they would be free from their responsibility of needing to "entertain" her. She and Nyondo could work on translation during the day and also have morning and evening services and teaching times.

But first she had to get approval from the field executive committee.

Permission was granted.

9

Chief Tanga

"Now that we're God's children," Tobacco asked, acting as group spokesman, "you're not going to abandon us as orphans, are you? Teach us more. There are five of us now on God's path. We meet together and 'read' the books you left with us. We talk about what we have learned, but others are asking questions we cannot answer. We need to be taught more. We need you to warn us of the evil and false things that will cause us to stumble. We need to learn how to walk with both feet on God's path."

It was time for Julie to tell them of her plan. She explained that her desire was to spend more time in their village, but that it was difficult because of the accommodations she was given. The owner of the house where she stayed was often away on trips and took the key with him! Also, when staying in someone else's house, it was awkward for Julie to spend her evenings typing what she and Nyondo had translated during the day. The typing needed to get done, but she didn't feel comfortable doing it while her hosts were trying to sleep. Secretly Julie also felt a need for space and privacy, but being in a culture where six people sleep in a room and *all* is shared, she chose not to say anything about it.

After stating her case, Julie sat back and listened as the villagers hashed it over among themselves. One woman understood. "She wants a house of her own," she told them. That was exactly what Julie wanted to hear.

As the weeks went by, more talking was done. Tobacco assured Julie that the villagers would work hard to build her a mud-walled translator's castle.

"We will all benefit from the Words of God you will translate among us and teach to us," he told her. "We will help you build."

Tobacco and his nephew decided where Julie's house would be built. It was the only vacant piece of land on their scenic hillside at the end of two neat rows of houses that trickled down the slope. All they had to do was check with the neighbor to make sure he had no other plans for the plot.

The neighbor's house was actually in the next "suburb" of the City-of-Bridges. His name was Tanga. He was the chief of the suburb. He agreed to Julie's house being built but he wasn't happy about it.

Chief Tanga, small in stature, was the leader of a comparably small domain—one tiny suburb of the City-of-Bridges. But the size of both himself and his village had no bearing on the regal way in which he commanded the respect of his villagers.

Ten years before Julie ever set foot in his village, Enoch and a Tsogo pastor had paid a visit.

"Get out of my village!" the chief ordered. "The Words of God will not be taught here. Get out!" The Bible teachers reluctantly retreated.

Six years passed and Enoch, armed with his new record player and Getsogo records, again visited Chief Tanga's village. He had taught each month in the neighboring suburbs of the City-of-Bridges and often wished he could cross the bridge to teach in Tanga's territory as well. He was sure that now curiosity would overcome pride and the chief would want to hear the machine that spoke his own language. Enoch was disappointed.

"I've told you before that in this village the Words of God will not be taught," Tanga stormed. "Look what they've done in other villages. The followers of those teachings no longer show respect to the old folks by dancing *bwiti* (the secret society dances, calling on the spirits) for them when they die. We respect our dead here. Get out!" Once again, Enoch retreated.

Four more years passed and Enoch returned a third time to Chief Tanga's domain, this time accompanied by Julie. The small chief could hardly be termed a gracious host, cutting off any thread of conversation that was started. But he did grudgingly call his villagers together and allowed the visitors to teach. When they prayed, however, he bowed neither his head nor his heart.

Several months later Julie was still making frequent visits to the City-of-Bridges and the leveling of the ground for her house was well underway. On one visit she took bars of laundry soap as thank-you gifts for some of the women who regularly brought her meals when she was staying in their village.

After the evening service Julie visited a couple homes to distribute her gifts. The first one was for Mandoh's wife. She was thrilled.

"Oh, sister of mine, come, let me bless you," she beamed. With that, she began spitting a fine spray. Luckily for Julie, she'd seen this special blessing once before, so she knew what she was supposed to do. She quickly tucked her hymnbook, Bible, flashlight and another cake of soap under her arms and held out her hands under the falling blessing! As vulgar as it sounds to the North American mind, in the Tsogo culture this was a wonderful thing. They don't bestow spittle on just anyone or for just any reason! This was a very special blessing.

Feeling highly honored, Julie made her way down the path to her next stop. When the lady of the house received her cake of soap, she broke into a spontaneous dance of joy. She whirled around her torch-lit room hugging the soap to her chest and singing about what a fortunate "mother" she was to have a "child" who would bring her a gift of cleanliness and riches! All that from a 20-cent bar of soap! Leaving that house, Julie decided to deliver the rest of her soap another day. She'd had about all the thanks she needed for one night!

At the end of the week as Julie was preparing to return home to Guevede, a messenger ran down the hillside and reported that Chief Tanga wanted to see her. She went, wondering what would prompt him to call for her, a teacher of the Words he continued to reject.

Leaving her suitcase where it was, she made her way to Tanga's house. She found him sitting with his family members around him. After greeting each one with a handshake, Julie sat down.

Tanga didn't waste any time getting down to business.

"I called you because I'm sick and I want to go to your village with you to be treated at your dispensary." He went on to explain that he hadn't stopped coughing for two months and now every cough had great pain to it. He didn't say anything about having tried every trick in the witch doctor's bag to heal the cough, but

Julie knew he would have gone through all the rites and ceremonies he knew. Still his illness remained and he now wanted to try "God's medicine," as the Guevede dispensary was called.

"Promise me you won't have anything else to do with sorcery," Julie bargained. "God will not mix His medicine with Satan's."

Tanga agreed.

As she walked back to pick up her luggage her mind was running ahead, wondering what God might be doing in Tanga's life. *Surely this must be the Lord's way of breaking through to him. Surely He will do a miracle and heal Tanga—body and soul—while he's at Guevede.*

Weeks passed and Chief Tanga's health returned. He went home on foot (a 38-kilometer/25-mile walk), detailing the wonderful treatment he received at the hands of the missionaries. He had gone to many services at the Guevede church and said he was planning to accept what he heard there.

Back home, Tanga's family agreed that he was much better, but they insisted that the treatment begun at the dispensary must be "completed." Tanga bowed to their pressure, going with them into the forest to resume the sorcery he knew he should leave behind.

On her next visit to Tanga's empire, Julie could not believe that the sick, bloated man she greeted was the same one who had walked away from the dispensary only a month earlier.

Her heart was heavy as the Christians told her how Tanga had returned to his old ways.

In the kitchen of Tanga's house, Julie abided by their custom and sat quietly as family members defended their decision to "complete" Tanga's treatment. Tanga said nothing, his glassy eyes looking down in shame. He knew he had done wrong. Finally, Julie had heard all she could take.

"I'm speaking," she declared, interrupting their excuses. She went back to the beginning and reviewed Tanga's sickness and his going to Guevede. Then she turned to Tanga.

"Did you say when you left Guevede, 'I am well and healed'? "

"I said that," he answered.

Addressing the kitchen full of people, Julie asked, "When he arrived here, didn't he arrive on his own feet, refusing to ride in the truck? Didn't he tell you he was well?"

"He did," they replied. "We heard him."

"How can you say then that he wasn't well when he came back?" Julie didn't wait for an answer. "You are mocking God," she continued. "You are making His work a plaything!" Tears began to roll down her cheeks. The family sat stunned. They had never seen a white woman cry.

"People of this village," Julie pleaded, "change your thoughts! Turn your hearts to God!" The tears continued to flow. Julie feared the villagers would interpret them as anger. "I have spoken," she choked out as she got up to leave.

Two days later Chief Tanga died—without Christ.

Julie would have loved to have written home that Tanga had accepted the Savior and given up his fetishes. But that wasn't the case.

Tanga's family asked her to transport his body to the place where he requested that he be buried, about 15 kilometers (10 miles) up a very poor road. She agreed. Six men accompanied her.

While they carried the coffin up the steep embankment, Julie stayed by the truck. She heard dirt hitting the coffin as the grave was closed. Tall trees reached toward heaven—Tanga's soul was not there. Vines swung from the trees, forming a green umbrella above her. The place where Julie stood was full of the beauty of God's hand—a God Tanga never acknowledged.

Back at the village, Julie's heart ached as she walked past her newly leveled land and looked toward Tanga's house. He wouldn't be her neighbor after all. She was discouraged, wondering if all her teaching was having any effect. It certainly hadn't done anything for Tanga.

The relentless beating of drums in the village that night served as a forceful reminder to Julie of just why she had come to Gabon. Death had once again made its uninvited appearance. The village women gathered together, tearing at their hair and clothes and crying out in mournful wails. What a sharp contrast to the victorious cry of Scripture: "Where, O death, is your victory? Where, O death, is your sting?" (1 Corinthians 15:55).

While the women mourned, the men of the village gathered in their meeting house. With fear-gripped hearts, they beat their drums through the night. Their calls and chants echoed back and forth across the hillside, calling out to the spirits.

Unable to block out neither the throbbing rhythm nor the woeful message of the drums, Julie shuddered at the blackness of the pagan soul, enshrouded by the terror of death. Yes, her heart often ached with loneliness for her family. But that was exceeded by an even greater ache for people trapped in darkness, that they would hear the liberating good news of Jesus Christ.

10

The Name on the Jacket

Julie carefully guided her truck loaded with baggage and people over 23 torturous kilometers (15 miles) from the government office at Mimongo to the central control post of Gabon's gold-mining area. The group had obtained a 10-day pass for ministry in the carefully controlled gold field. They were on their way to the Dibua (DEEB-wa) people, a Tsogo clan considered even more backward than the rest of the tribe.

This trip had been planned for nearly two years. In March of 1970, a group from the Dibua clan had passed through the City-of-Bridges where they stayed over night. Pastor Joel and Julie were there at the time and Joel had played for them the Getsogo gospel records.

"Those are good records with true matters on them," they said. "Those aren't at all like the devil's records that we play in our village on our record player. We want to hear more of those true words."

Pastor Joel told them that perhaps a group of Guevede believers would be able to make a trip to Dibua country in dry season to teach them of Jesus. One of the Dibua men told Pastor Joel the name of his village.

"When your group is ready to come, you let us know, and we'll be ready for you," he had said.

Pastor Joel wrote the man's name and village on a record jacket and agreed that he would write to him. As they parted, the man said, "You took my address. That means we've finalized this agreement. You've made us Dibua people a promise. Do not break your promise."

Finally, nearly two years later, in January 1972, the evangelism team went for the first time over the twists, turns and tumbles of the road to Dibua country. Pastor Joel had arranged the trip, recruiting five believers from the Guevede church to come along, as well as Julie, Anita Reader and himself.

The group made their headquarters in the guest house of the regional head chief. He didn't seem to care what they had come for, but out of duty allowed them to stay. Services were held morning and evening in the surrounding villages.

In this remote part of the country, white people were seldom seen, especially two at a time! And never had they heard a white person speak

Getsogo! Julie enjoyed the wonder and confusion that her use of their words caused. It was a small but beautiful reward for the countless hours she had spent plugging away at language study.

Three days and several services into the trip, an invitation to accept Jesus as Savior was given for the first time ever among the Dibua. Twenty people responded, saying they wanted to make a break with their old ways and to walk on God's path. One of them was an old lady who told how her husband's relatives had tried to kill her. In her dying breath she had called out, "God, are you there? God, am I a person You are going to allow to die like this or an animal that You don't care for?"

A few days later she began to recover. Now she knew why God gave her back her physical life even though she did not know how to address Him or what to ask Him for. He'd done it so that she could also gain spiritual life. She enthusiastically accepted the message of Jesus Christ, not wanting the opportunity to slip by.

The next day, the team went on to Mebe village where God showed them again that He was in control of the timing of their trip. They had just finished the evening teaching session and were about to sit down to a meal of porcupine, hot peppers and manioc (a starchy root), when three men came asking them to bring injections and medicine because a man was seriously ill.

"We do not have any medicine," Julie told them, "but we will go with you."

They set off across the village. On the way they found out that the man had been in a drunken stupor when he fell headfirst onto a cement floor. Since that moment he hadn't opened his eyes, spoken or moved and seemed to be dying in spite of the day and night dancing that had been done for him. It was now the fourth night since his fall.

They entered the room where the sick man lay. One of his wives was sitting beside him on the bed.

"Give him a needle, please, please," she pled.

"We don't have needles or medicine," Julie told her, "but we do have the authority to ask Almighty God to heal him."

The man's relatives hesitated. This was not what they were expecting to hear.

Pastor Joel spoke.

"You admitted that your sorcery did not raise this man from his bed. I want to tell you that there is a God in heaven who controls this man's days and knows the number of them. Perhaps He will say that this man's days are not expired and will grant him healing and life."

The relatives held a council and agreed that their sorcery had failed. Perhaps they should allow the people of God to invoke their source of power.

Pastor Joel explained further.

"We also want you to know that Almighty God will not mix His power with that of the sorceror. You must promise that if we ask God to heal this man, you will not do any more of your rites."

More discussion followed. The family gave their promise.

Pastor Joel and George, another member of the team, prayed for the dying man.

The next morning before gathering the villagers for a service, the Guevede group went to visit the sick man. They found him lying with his eyes open. With signs and a few words he indicated that he felt pain in various places. Again Pastor Joel led the group in prayer, thanking God for the work He had begun and asking Him to complete it.

By evening the man was sitting on the edge of his bed, able to understand conversation, but still speaking only a few words.

Another night passed. The man was able to get up and walk to the house where his relatives had gathered. Superstitious villagers said that the two white women had raised the man from near death. The Guevede team denied it, pointing out that it had been two black men who had prayed for the man's healing.

"It is Almighty God, the God whom we have come to tell you about, who healed this man," they declared.

"It is God," the sick man proclaimed loudly. "It is God." Later that day, Pastor Joel showed his team a Getsogo record. On the jacket of the record was written: "Masembo Francois, village: Mebe." That was the name of the man who had extended the invitation to Pastor Joel to come to Mebe. It was also the name of the man who, a few houses away, lay recovering from a serious concussion!

Pastor Joel was excited. "By inviting us to come to his village with the message of God, that man saved his life nearly two years before the accident happened."

The people of Mebe recognized that something supernatural had happened. It wasn't so much that they were amazed by the miracle. They had seen sorcerors pull people back from the brink of death before. But what they marveled at was that where the sorceror failed, God came in and raised the man up. They had never heard of of anything like that!

Now many villagers came to hear what the visitors were teaching. Once again an invitation to leave the old ways and walk on God's path was given. This time 30 adults received Jesus as their Savior—the first time they heard of Him.

The next evening while waiting for supper to cook, Julie browsed through a few copies of the *Alliance Witness* (now *Alliance Life*). They were several months old. Having traveled by boat mail, they had arrived at Guevede just before the group left on their Dibua trip.

One of the missions prayer requests jumped off the page at Julie. It was for Pastor Joel and members of the Guevede church who were planning a two-week evangelistic trip into the Dibua area.

"That's it!" exclaimed Pastor Joel, eyes wet with emotion. "That's why we're seeing the Dibua come to Christ the first time they hear of Him. Around the world, wherever that magazine has gone, people have prayed."

And God had answered.

11

The Trials of Translation

Five years had passed since Julie and Nyondo began their translation work. Now in November 1974, Dr. Wilson of the British and Foreign Bible Societies paid a visit to Gabon. He was impressed with the caliber of work Julie and Nyondo were doing. If they continued with this quality, he said, the translation was sure to be accepted for printing.

However, all his news was not good. Julie was hoping that at least part of Nyondo's salary would be paid by the Bible Society, relieving the financial burden on the field's translation fund. In only one year, Gabon's minimum wage had doubled and it was expected to jump another 25 percent in the next few months. The Mission needed funding from the Bible Society.

"We would love to offer financial assistance," Dr. Wilson said, "but the Society is suffering financially due to a shortage of paper and its high cost when it is available, as well as countless other expenses. I regret to tell you that you should not expect to receive any financial help for the Getsogo translation." Dr. Wilson also advised that Julie and Nyondo should be very selective about what they spent their time translating so that if the program would grind to a halt, the most essential books would at least be in mimeographed form.

What a blow! Could it be that after going this far, the project wouldn't be completed? Could it be that, in her confidence that God desired the whole New Testament to be in Getsogo, Julie had misinterpreted His plan? Or could it be that He would supply their needs in an unexpected way?

Following Dr. Wilson's advice, Julie and Nyondo continued on with their translation, carefully prioritizing the passages. Frequently they went to the City-of-Bridges where Julie stayed in her tiny translation house the villagers built for her. She left a barrel full of her belongings there—dishes, bedding, etc., making her "home away from home" a comfortable place to live and work. Between morning and evening teaching times, Julie and Nyondo labored to get as many verses translated as they could. But time was running out.

By February there had been no word of financial help from the Bible Society. The translation fund was four months behind and

Nyondo had yet to be paid for his last month of work. A few gifts from friends and family in North America arrived, but they were not enough to save the project. Over $2,000 in wages alone was needed to complete the translation. A decision was made that they would work until the end of March, at which time there would be no alternative but to lay Nyondo off.

A few days later Julie made her weekly trip to pick up the mail. In the box were a six-month-old copy of the Abbotsford newspaper, several pieces of mail for others in the village and one letter from the International Bible Society.

With heart racing, Julie tore open the letter. Surely this was the news they were hoping for. The translation project would carry on after all.

As her eyes scanned the page, Julie's heart fell. The letter was to inform her of a change in policy regarding printing for smaller tribes. Formerly the size of the tribe was no object. If the congregations were enthusiastic and backed the translation and if the work met certain standards, the Bible Society supported it, even though the cost per copy was high. But due to financial constraints, that policy was now being modified.

In light of the size of the Tsogo Christian community and their proposed initial printing of only 1,500 copies of the New Testament, the cost would be prohibitive. The letter suggested that they should plan to have a mimeographed New Testament after all.

"God, what's going on?" Julie questioned. "What are You doing? After all this, are we going to be left with only portions of the New Testament run off on an old mimeograph machine?"

Julie started a letter to several churches and individuals in Canada and the U.S., informing her family and friends of the financial needs the translation project was facing. Watching the steam rise from the jungle following an afternoon downpour, she wondered if she should even bother to finish the letter.

Why even write it? she asked herself. *We need way more money than we'll ever see. And even if we can finish the translation, we have no way to get it printed.*

After supper that evening she walked into her office. The half-written letter was still rolled in her typewriter.

"Why not?" she asked aloud. "We've got nothing to lose. I don't want to lay Nyondo off without at least making people at home aware of the need." The letter went in the mail.

Pastor Joel couldn't accept the thought of the translation not being completed. He introduced the idea of a "subscription" fee for those who saw the need and subscribed to the idea of having the Scriptures in their own language. It was decided that each subscriber would pay the equivalent of 50 cents, or whatever he or she could afford, as a vote for the translation to continue. These offerings would go toward Nyondo's pay.

Meanwhile, on the other side of the ocean, people started to give to the Getsogo translation project. In the month of March alone, $1,814 was received.

When Julie received the financial statement for March, she cried tears of joy. She was speechless, unable to express the gratitude she felt. Translation did not need to stop after all! In one month, people had given nearly enough money see the project through.

There was still the unanswered question of the printing costs. Would the Bible Society print it or could another printer be located? Either way, the overwhelming response from believers in Canada and the U.S. fanned into flame the hope that a printed Getsogo New Testament would someday be a reality.

A month later, still feeling warmed by the steady flame of confidence in what God could do, Julie received another financial statement. April's giving was $3,212! More joyful tears! More thank-you letters!

When the Guevede believers heard of the response of their brothers and sisters whom they had never met, they were inspired to give more as well. One young man who was perpetually unemployed stood up.

"If people in another country who don't even know what my language says can give gifts of money for God's writings to be turned into my language, then surely I, who was born crying that language, am obliged to give also," he said. "Here's my part."

The translation fund was now sufficient to pay Nyondo through the end of the project as well as covering the costs of mimeographing each book as it was translated. And there would be funds left over for the final printing.

Obviously the Almighty God wanted His Word in Getsogo too.

12

With Both Feet

Julie sat on a crowded bench in Mandoh's living room for the evening service at the City-of-Bridges. She had arrived late that afternoon, along with Nyondo and Ngonde and Pastor Joel, for five days of teaching and translation.

Just a few miles out of Guevede they had spent 45 minutes with the truck high-centered on a mound of dirt in the middle of the road while all four wheels spun in the mud-filled ruts on either side. The men were thankful for the tools that Julie always carried when she traveled as they shoveled and scraped dirt out from under the truck and put it under the wheels.

As Julie watched, listening to the animal cries from the forest as if they were laughing at this predicament, she was grateful it was only mud. She thought back to the bitter cold prairie winters of her childhood, remembering the sight of people shoveling their cars out of mountainous snow drifts. *This may not be pleasant,* she thought as she watched the dirt fly from the shovels and splash into the mud, *but at least no one has ever frozen to death in a mud puddle!*

Back on the road again, Julie and the others inched and slid their way to the City-of-Bridges in time for a quick meal and an evening service. They were encouraged by the attendance. Services in the City-of-Bridges were always somewhat entertaining since the people hadn't yet learned proper church behavior.

One of the villagers was asked to pray. He asked the Lord to intervene in various situations. Others interrupted and corrected him so he'd get his prayer straight. After several more minutes he was interrupted again. "It's time to say, 'In the name of Jesus, Amen,' " the impatient listener told him.

Later in the service, as the offering was being collected, three dogs in the house began snapping and snarling at each other, and then progressed to an all-out fight. In a room crowded with 28 adults and 10 children, there wasn't much space to get out of their way! Eventually the dogs got outside, the people got back in, the offering was collected and the service carried on.

It was late that night when Julie blew out the lamp in her tiny house. She was so glad she and the others hadn't allowed the bad roads to discourage them from coming. For almost a year it had seemed as if the church there was

Julie Fehr, graduation from Canadian Bible College, 1964.

The Christian and Missionary Alliance Church at Guevede.

The house on the Guevede mission station where Julie lived for nearly 20 years.

Tobacco in his old military coat.

Stuck in the mud. "But at least no one has ever frozen to death in a mud puddle!"

One of the river crossings leading to the City-of-Bridges.
The vine lying on the logs was, at one time, a handrail.

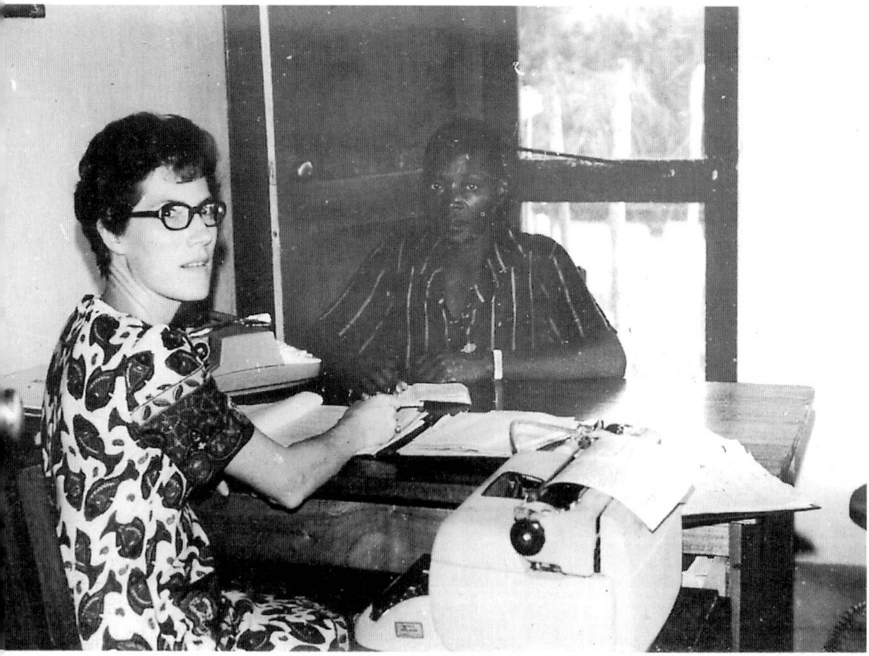

Julie and Nyondo working on translation.

The view from Julie's house in the City-of-Bridges.

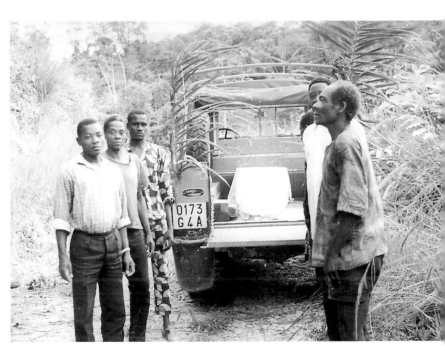

Julie's vehicle became a funeral hearse when Chief Tanga died.
Nyondo is on the far left.

Pallbearers taking Chief Tanga's casket to its burial place.

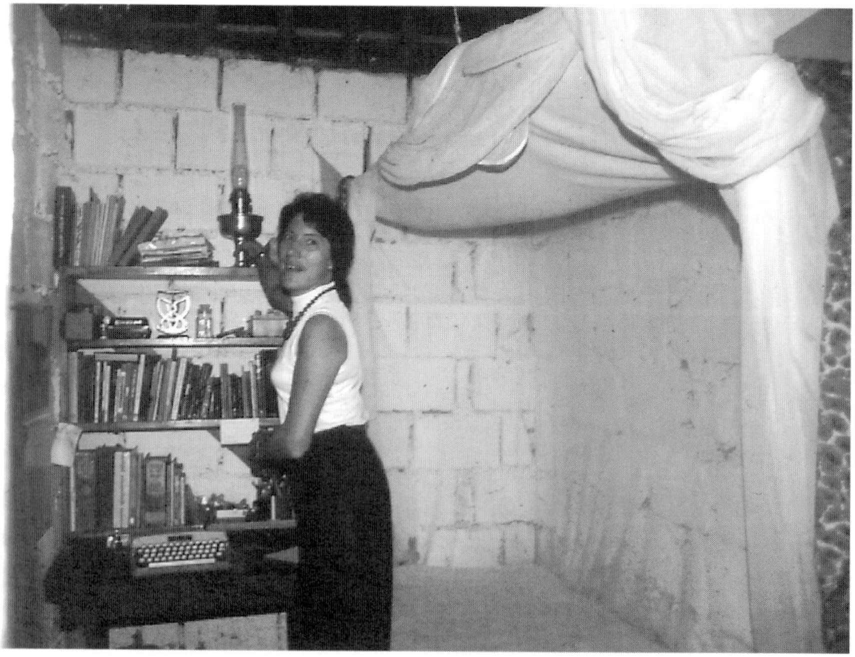

The small translation house in the City-of-Bridges.
The "curtain" is actually a mosquito net tied up for the day.

One of the villages in the Dibua area where the team from Guevede held evangelistic services.

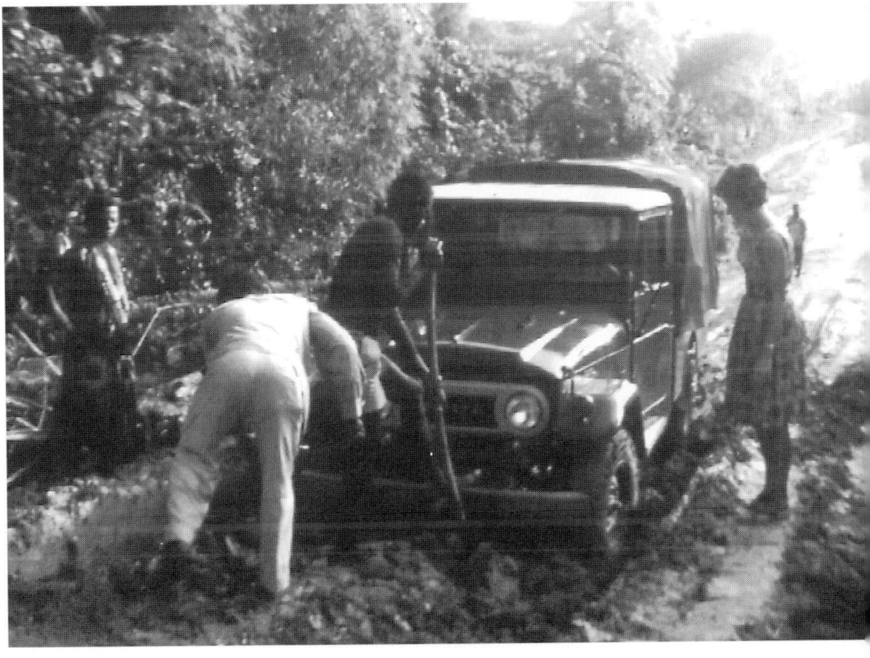

Travel during the rainy season is difficult. Large trucks make deep ruts and smaller vehicles are easily high-centered.

Villagers gathered for a house meeting.

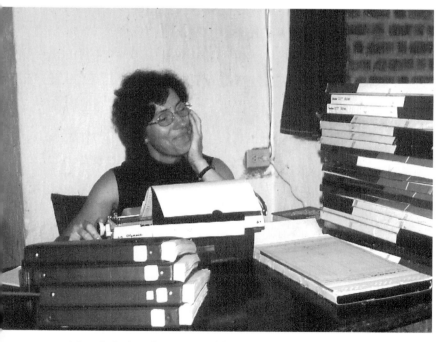

A break during the typing of the Getsogo New Testament.
Note stack of stencil boxes.

Anita Reader cranks the manually-run mimeograph machine.

Collating pages of the freshly mimeographed Getsogo New Testament.

R to L: Julie, Anita Reader, Nyondo and another helper, each holding one copy of the mimeographed New Testament.

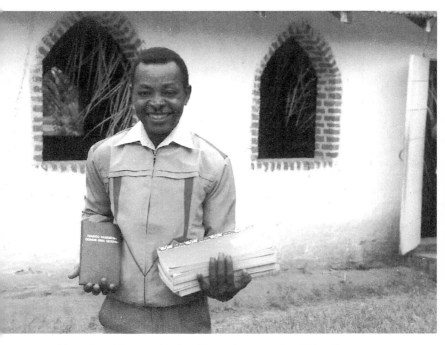

Nyondo with two-thirds of the mimeographed New Testament in his left hand and the printed edition in his right hand.

"Air Canada" and its pilot.

Pastor Joel in the Guevede church at the dedication of the Getsogo New Testament, 1985.

Canadian friend, Joan Carter, joins Julie on the beach in Libreville during a 1989 visit.

Enjoying a picnic with Lisa Rohrick in 1992.

At a TEE retreat in Libreville, 1991.

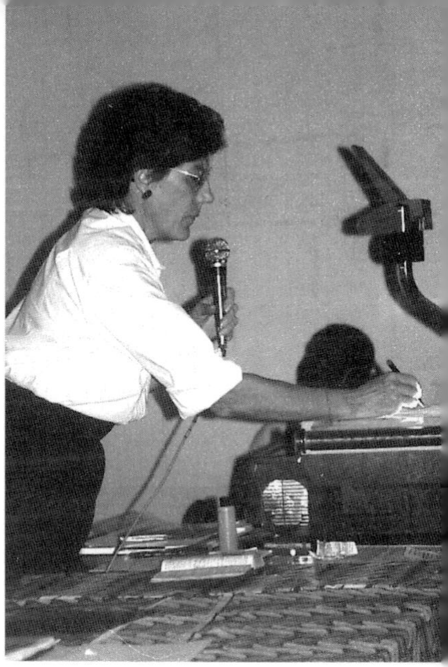

Teaching at a TEE seminar in Cote d'Ivoire, 1992.

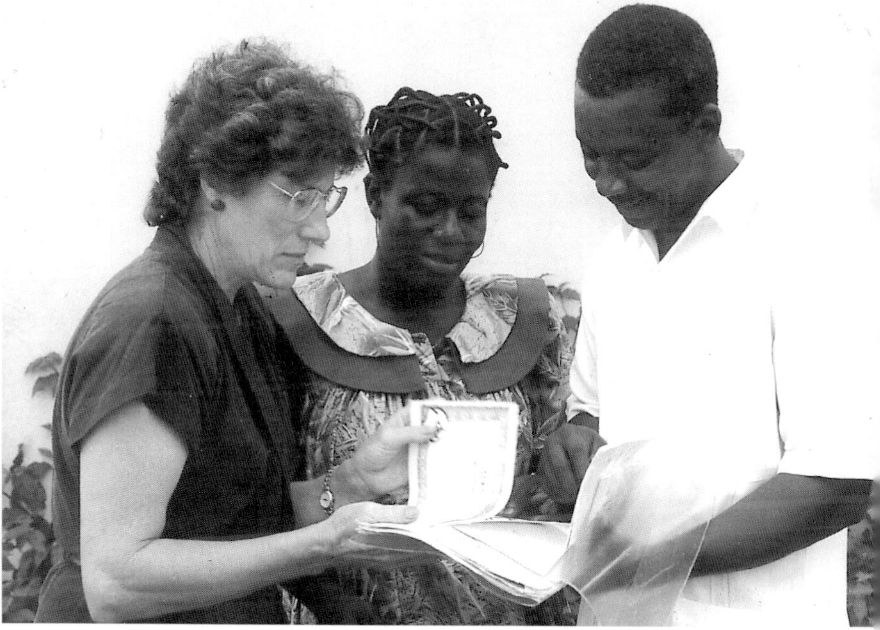

Felix and Suzanne, a couple involved in TEE lay ministry check out materials.

Avea II Alliance Church in Libreville.
Tarpaulins shelter the overflow crowds.

The home of the Bethel Bible Institute and TEE/Gabon.

Julie's last prayer card, 1992.

At the airport in São Paulo, Brazil, March, 1994, nearing the end of her around-the-world trip.

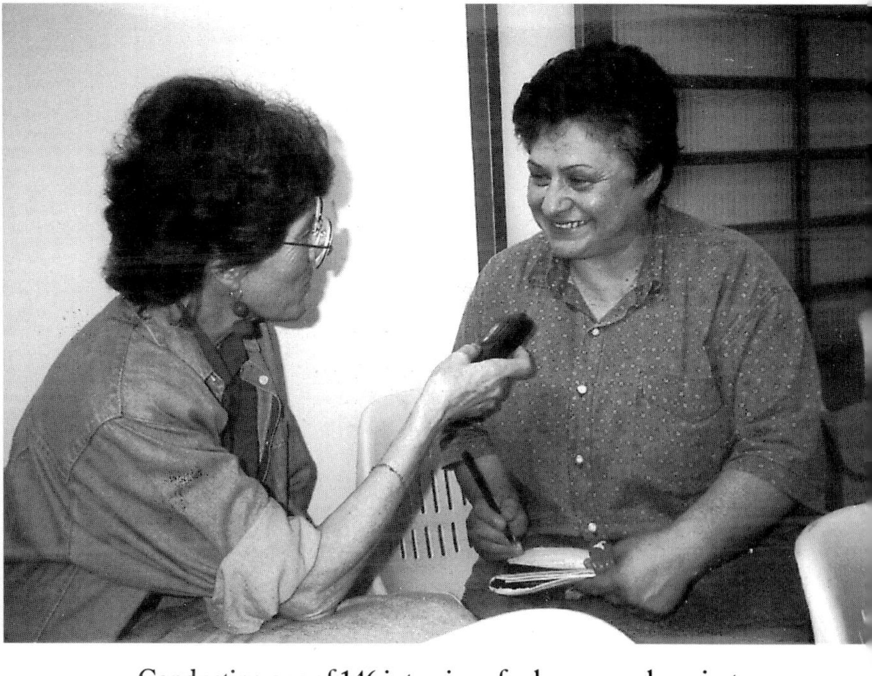

Conducting one of 146 interviews for her research project at the Billy Graham Center.

Judy Milne, Lisa Rohrick, Julie Fehr and Joan Carter, July 17, 1994.
Taken in North York General Hospital in Toronto, Canada
the morning Julie was transferred to Langley, British Columbia.

coming to a standstill. There had been no new faces at the services and many of the familiar faces came and went between rites and ceremonies at night and God's Word during the day. They were trying to walk with one foot on God's path and one foot on the other. It was disheartening.

But things were starting to turn around. The crowd that evening was the biggest she'd seen in a while. They interrupted and asked questions as Julie taught from Scripture that had been translated just that week. And when she asked them questions there was a lively response. God had not forgotten this isolated collection of villages deep in Gabon's tropical rain forest after all.

The Sunday morning service began at 7 a.m. After a Bible lesson, the believers made their way, singing and clapping, through the village down to the river bank for a baptismal service. All who wanted to watch were invited to come along. Nearly 100 adults lined both sides of the river to watch this strange new custom.

Pastor Joel stood at the water's edge explaining why each of the six people to be baptized would be fully immersed in the river. By obeying Jesus' example and command, these people were saying that they desired to follow Him and to stay on His path.

All of the baptismal candidates told the crowd of onlookers what Jesus had done in their lives and why they wanted to be baptized.

The highlight for Julie was Tobacco, the one who had opened the door to the City-of-Bridges for her translation and teaching ministry. He told how fear had once gripped his heart and how he used to seek guidance from the spirits, how he learned that his old ways were of the devil, but now he was walking on God's path, free from fear.

With much singing and clapping the service continued. Fetishes which had been turned over to Pastor Joel were burned, symbolizing that their previous owners would be forever free from their power. One of the objects to be thrown in the fire was Tobacco's pipe which had been part of his life for years. He had not given it up when he initially burned his fetishes. But now, declaring that "Tobacco" was not really his name, but only a nickname, he admitted the pipe had controlled him long enough and he would not use it again.

Some believers were distressed that so many sacred objects were burned. Such total destruction would surely anger the spirits that lived in the fetishes and therefore the objects should merely be thrown into the river to float away. But Pastor Joel reminded his audience that God's power far surpasses that of the spirits and that Christians should not live in fear of fetishes or the spirits possessing them. When all the fetishes were thoroughly burned, the ashes were scooped up and thrown into the river so that no sorcerer could make any use of them.

The service concluded with prayer. Nyondo prayed for those who had just been baptized. He asked God to protect them and keep them strong. "God, make their hearts as steady as a boulder in a roaring river," he prayed.

Julie echoed that prayer in her heart, thinking mostly of the young people. There were so many forces begging for their attention, trying to sweep them away with the rushing current. Julie loved the time she spent learning from the village elders. But her heart was burdened for the 50 percent of Gabon's population under 20 years old—young people caught between two cultures.

Many teenagers wanted nothing to do with the old customs, not even caring to use their mother tongue. They were drawn to the new customs instituted by the laws of their newly independent land. (Gabon received its independence from France in 1960.) They wanted to be able to read and speak fluently in French, the language that depicted progress and intelligence. Yet French was still foreign to them and the European customs even more so.

In church, school and town, teens were expected to be a part of the new Gabon. In their homes, the village and the forest, they were required to be obedient to the laws of the past. Many of the customs from the past were good—stories, parables, weaving, hunting, etc. But neither the teens nor the adults seemed able to distinguish between the profitable customs and the harmful ones such as initiation rites, sorcery and promiscuity.

Many young people alternately laughed at and dabbled in the old customs. They wanted to be modern and embrace new imported ways. But, like stiff leather shoes on habitually bare, trail-worn feet, the new ways did not fit well. Julie recognized that in any culture a teenager stands between two worlds—that of childhood and that of adulthood. But she saw Gabon's teens being pulled in four directions—two age-wise and two culture-wise. And they stood confused in the center of it all.

One dark night there was a knock at Julie's door. As she invited M'Bombe in, she wondered if he came at night because he didn't want his buddies to see him. Or perhaps it seemed too long to wait until the next daylight? M'Bombe asked his questions, like Nicodemus who came to Jesus at night, expressing his doubts and reservations. And on this night Jesus was making the same demand of M'Bombe that He made of Nicodemus—he must renounce the only way of life he knew. Julie knew it was a lot to ask of a teen, but she also knew that everyone has to choose between Jesus and the world, that no one can serve two masters.

M'Bombe could have turned away from Christ's demands. Jesus would have let him. But instead, M'Bombe prayed, "Forgive me, Savior. I've come before and I'm coming again. You're asking a lot—You always do. But You never ask more than I can give. So I'll give myself. Here, take."

He stepped out of Julie's office, welcomed back into the darkness by the beat of drums. Julie couldn't tell if the drums were real or if it was their transistor counterpart pulsing from village radios. Either way, the thumping call was the same. It symbolized the strange near-fusion of African and Western paganism. It symbolized the struggle in every teen who wanted to follow Jesus. On one hand there was the desire to yield to the rhythm of life in which they grew up. And on the other, there was the desire to fight, for Christ's sake, against the very pulse-beat of their jungle heritage.

Julie's involvement in youth work increased. She became the president of the youth work committee, responsible for planning and directing annual youth camps. There was nothing quite as exciting to her as hearing a room full of 20 girls—who were supposed to be sleeping—sing praise songs while moonlight filtered through the partially opened window shutter.

At the final meeting of one camp, the teens were given an opportunity to share what God had taught them. One boy stood up and told the group, "I was walking two paths at once—or trying to. But if you begin walking with one foot on each trail, how many kilometers can you go? Five? No! One? No! The paths move farther and farther apart and you can no longer keep one foot in each path. That was my problem, so I put both feet on the easiest path. I quit trying to be on God's path at all. I was wrong. Now I see I need to be on God's path. That's where I want to be—with both feet!"

God was working in lives, showing Himself to be more powerful than the spirits of darkness.

13

The End of the World

The translation was finished! It was March 30, 1976, when Nyondo and Julie translated the final verse of the New Testament into Getsogo several weeks ahead of the deadline they had set for themselves.

That didn't mean their work was finished, but it was one giant step closer. There was still typing to do, and more typing, and then more typing after that. Everything they had translated needed to be typed onto stencils so that it could be mimeographed and then circulated among the literate believers for their use and correction.

Julie got to work typing her share of the stencils while Nyondo worked on his. She put in 10 or 12 hours on days when she could free herself from other responsibilities. By the end of June her part was completed.

The annual conference of the Gabon missionaries was in June that year. It is at annual conference where business and ministry decisions are made, such as which missionaries are assigned to which towns. The 1976 conference decided to appoint Julie and Anita Reader to Mimongo for the following year.

Mimongo, the government administrative center for the district, was 60 kilometers (40 miles) from Guevede. At that time it had neither a church nor a pastor, but there was a small nucleus of believers with whom services were held once a month. Julie and Anita's assignment was to work with those believers in establishing a permanent church. Julie still had work to do on the Getsogo New Testament before it could be printed, but she was no longer tied down to an eight-hour day of translating. She was excited about the possibilities in Mimongo.

No housing was available in Mimongo, but there was a vacant parsonage building in the village of Seka Seka only three-and-a-half miles away. It had a new thatch roof which made it clean and cool. The walls were earth brick which the girls brightened up with some whitewash. Painting mud brick was quite a challenge—it was like painting on sand. A few strokes and the paintbrush was full of dirt from the wall. The white paint turned to cream, to beige, to brown, to something gritty and unmanageable. So Anita and Julie did the modern art thing. They soaked up all the paint their brushes would hold and then shook them at the wall as if it were a canvas, splattering it with streaks, dots and sloshes of white. Eventually whole walls were covered and their work of art dried fresh and clean.

Julie and Anita were the first white people to live in Seka Seka. Their daily routine caused lots of excitement for the children who wondered and exclaimed at all the fascinating things they were witnessing. As Julie sat working at her typewriter, she was only inches away from a living curtain of woolly heads that moved up and down in her window and analyzed her every move. When she paused for a moment and looked straight ahead, thinking of what she would write next, she heard the kids say, "Oh, look, now she's praying!"

Now that they were living in the village and not just guests for a few days, Julie and Anita were expected to do the visiting and greeting that village women did. Julie loved visiting in their kitchens and offering a bench to those who came to visit in hers. But the greeting was quite another thing.

The important greeting happened immediately after sunrise each morning. On rainy days it could be postponed until 6:30 or 7:00, but on a bright and cloudless morning they needed to be up and dressed by 5:45 or 6:00 in order to greet their neighbors. Otherwise the village population would think they were hostile, sick or away on a trip!

Morning greetings didn't do much for starting one's day with time alone with God. So, if you can't beat them, join them! Julie sat at her open window each morning, facing the village, her Bible open on her lap. Anyone who passed by got a greeting, and when they asked her what she was doing, she told them that she liked to greet God in the morning before she greeted people! They understood that and went on their way.

Ministry in Mimongo was exciting. The town was considered to be the "end of the world," the last place that government officials wanted to be assigned. Its out-of-the-way location, coupled with the fact that there had never been a Protestant church there before, nor a pastor, nor a missionary, made it a place for prodigal Christians to hide. They felt safe in Mimongo, and, with time, they even managed to escape their consciences.

As Julie spent time in Mimongo, she found more and more of these runaway Christians. Sooner or later their consciences would get the better of them and they would introduce themselves as believers.

The group was beginning to grow in numbers but they did not have a central meeting place. They were given a lot on which to build an evangelism center, with meeting rooms and residences for a pastor and missionary. While a number of Gabon's trees were being used up in paper work, the Mimongo building project was at a standstill. But that did not mean the church itself was at a standstill, since the

Church of Jesus Christ does not consist of buildings, but of people. Julie's work was mostly one-on-one, spending time with individuals.

She also started a pre-baptism class. Two attended the first class—a high school teacher and his teenage daughter. That number didn't increase. On Easter Sunday Paul and Christine were baptized in the river flowing through Mimongo.

Many curious onlookers joined the singing processional as they made their way from the schoolroom church to the river's edge. Before they were baptized, Christine spoke briefly, and then Paul told how God had spoken to him through an ordinary village incident.

An old man had to go and "redeem" his goat which had been caught eating garden produce in a nearby village. The older man came to Paul to borrow money to buy back his goat. The sum was considerable. Paul began to think, *All that money to redeem a goat—a goat which has little value or significance—and yet it's important enough to its owner that he is going to great pains to reclaim it.*

Then Paul thought of his own life. *Who owns me?* he wondered. *And what price would be needed to redeem a person?* He remembered a Christian friend telling him that Jesus came to redeem men and women. He was relieved to find out that the total price had been paid for him—it had cost Jesus His life. All he had to do was commit himself to the ownership of Jesus Christ, his Redeemer. Now, by water baptism, he was publicly declaring his commitment to walk on God's path.

God was building His Church in Mimongo, one brick at a time.

14

Down to the Wire

The following year, 1977, the Gabon field conference decided that Julie and Anita would move back to Guevede. Julie still went to Mimongo periodically to take her turn teaching, but the bulk of the work there was turned over to another missionary returning from furlough. Once again Julie was back behind her desk working on the Getsogo New Testament.

Mimeographed copies of the New Testament had been circulated to several literate believers. As they used them, they made notes of things that were incorrect, unclear or could be improved. Now it was time for Julie and Nyondo to take all those suggestions and incorporate them into a revision of the Getsogo New Testament.

A committee of seven believers met every Thursday to read together and work on various questions that came up. It was a tedious job.

When heads began to nod, Julie often pulled out her notebook of questions and got a lively discussion going.

A meeting with a representative from the Bible Society was arranged in Libreville. Nyondo and his wife Ngonde rode with Julie over the 500 dusty and rut-filled kilometers (330 miles) to the capital city where Mr. Fehderau was to join them.

They met planes. He wasn't on them. They haunted the post office. There was no mail. For two weeks they stayed in Libreville with no sign of him and no word telling why there was no sign of him! Disappointed, they returned to Guevede with their briefcase full of unanswered questions. A few weeks later, a letter came explaining that Gabon hadn't granted him a visa, so he was unable to keep the appointment.

More calendar pages turned. Julie and friends were well into the revision with the tedious typings and re-typings that entailed. The committee was now meeting on Tuesdays as well as Thursdays to speed up the process, and Julie was still trying to meet with a consultant from the Bible Society. Another meeting was arranged. This time the plan was for Julie and Nyondo to fly to Cameroon where Mr. Fehderau would meet them.

In January 1978, after sailing through the red tape of obtaining visas, Julie and Nyondo boarded an Air Gabon plane headed for

Cameroon. Julie didn't sleep well that night, anticipating meeting in just a few hours with a man whose word could determine whether or not the Getsogo New Testament would be printed. It was the final evaluation of all that she and Nyondo had labored over for several years. If he didn't approve, all that work would be for nothing!

For the next five days, Julie and Nyondo worked with Mr. Fehderau for nine or 10 hours a day. He questioned them on what they had done and why they had chosen to translate certain words and phrases the way they had. Julie and Nyondo were able to explain and justify what they had done and received a great deal of affirmation and encouragement.

They also received just what they had been hoping for—verbal confirmation that the Getsogo New Testament would be printed and instructions to prepare for that printing. A Christian press had been located in Hong Kong. They would do the printing at a lower cost. The relatively small press run was no longer a problem. God was opening the door. They were on the home stretch of the Getsogo translation project!

Back in Gabon, Julie and Nyondo wasted no time in getting to work. There were 10 months of work yet to be done and only five months in which to do it. The whole New Testament had to be typed, proofread several times, typed onto stencils, proofread again, corrected, mimeographed and assembled before the first of August when Julie was to leave Gabon for furlough.

"I know I work best with deadlines," Julie told her colleagues, "but isn't this just a little ridiculous?"

"We won't say it cannot be done," they replied, not wanting to discourage her. "But let's say it's never been done that we know of!"

Julie felt like she'd taken on the job of ringmaster in a three-ring circus. In Ring #1 was the local committee, consisting of Pastor Joel, several laymen and Nyondo (with Julie entering the ring when time allowed), juggling ideas and meanings as they worked on the final stages.

To the side of the same ring, just keeping ahead of them, Julie checked the translation against a French "source" translation to make sure they had not inadvertently skipped a verse or verse number or even an entire paragraph.

Ring #2 featured Nyondo at the typewriter (except the two days a week he met with the committee). His job was to type up a "dummy" copy of the New Testament from what the committee (and time and usage) had corrected. Julie could also be seen running in and out of Ring #2 in her "spare" time, assisting Nyondo with proofreading. Anita was also one of the performers in this ring, where she made her entrance following her morning's work at the dispensary to do proofreading alongside Pastor Joel.

In Ring #3 of the "translation circus" Julie spent most of her time typing the final manuscript of the Getsogo New Testament onto stencils which would be mimeographed and a copy sent to the Hong Kong printer. She was hot on the heels of Nyondo and the proofreaders doing the dummy copy, who were hot on the heels of the corrections committee, who were breathing down Julie's neck as she compared the new translation with the source copy!

The sound of typing echoed around the Guevede hill day after day, week after week. Julie finished checking with the source translation, the committee finished their reading and discussing of vocabulary. Still the typewriters rattled out their pages.

One sunny June afternoon, one of the typewriters stopped.

"Monyepi, I am finished! Praise the Lord!" Nyondo called out, removing the last page of the New Testament "dummy" from the carriage of his typewriter. That called for a break! And a celebration! There was still some proofreading and a lot of typing to do, but Nyondo and Julie enjoyed a few minutes of reflection.

Day after day, word by word, the New Testament had been translated into Getsogo. They prayed together, thanking God for what He had done, both of them marveling at how obviously it was His work. Nyondo, uneducated in French or formal schooling, was chosen with

Julie knowing little about him except that he had a spiritual warmth and love for Jesus. Julie was untrained as a translator but had a love for the Getsogo language and an awareness of its richness. Both had been prepared by God. The result was the New Testament in Getsogo. And it was nearly finished!

Back to the typing!

Julie continued typing stencils 12 to 13 hours a day, six days a week, surprised that she had the stamina to keep going. Anita spent the same number of hours standing beside a manually run mimeograph machine, turning its handle around and around. With the steady click of the machine, pages of the Getsogo New Testament appeared.

One young student came to help proofread. "Wow! That's it!" he exclaimed, reading with a French New Testament in one hand and a "wet-from-the-press" Getsogo page in the other. "That's exactly it!"

Julie and Anita kept working.

It was July 13, 1978. The machines were quiet and everyone was asleep—everyone except Julie, that is. The cries of the cicadas cut into the night air. Fireflies sat outside the window in their bright halos, blinking their Morse code across the darkened window screen. Julie felt like she was imitating them as she sat in the circle of light from her kerosene lamp. A few hours earlier she had finished typing the last page of Revelation. There remained a few days of mimeographing and collating ahead, but the typing was finished. Tears of joy filled Julie's eyes and rolled slowly down her cheeks. The entire Getsogo New Testament was finally on stencils and most of it had been run off. She was too excited to sleep.

Two weeks later, Julie boarded an Air Afrique plane for France, en route to Canada. In her big handbag were 10 pounds of pages of the Getsogo New Testament (850 double-spaced pages). In her suitcase were another 10 pounds of pages—a reserve copy to be stored in Canada, should anything happen to the master copy in transit to the Bible Society in England.

Gratitude and relief flooded Julie's heart. All those years of work were behind her. She now held in her hands a manuscript ready for printing. Someday soon each Tsogo believer could own their own copy of the "Writings of God."

15

Fishing the Right Way

During her furlough year, Julie was approached by the director of The Christian and Missionary Alliance in Africa about the possibility of heading up a Theological Education by Extension (TEE) program for Gabon. After some serious thought and prayer, she agreed to accept the challenge, though she felt both fearful and incapable. All she knew about TEE was that it had been brought up before and the national Church of Gabon had vetoed it as a program that "would never work." She also knew that some of her missionary colleagues were not too keen about the idea, which didn't do much to calm her fears!

Furlough was fast becoming a memory, while God worked on Julie's fears. She received a letter from the Bible school committee in Gabon. The Bethel Bible School had been closed for several years due to lack of students. Perhaps a program that would take Bible training to the people would fill the need for training leaders for the national Church. In their annual meeting, the committee decided that TEE would be an arm of Bethel Bible School and recommended that it be put into operation as soon as possible.

The next thing to be taken care of was Julie's own ignorance. She didn't know much of anything about TEE, let alone how to get a brand-new program off the ground. The Alliance Division of Overseas Ministries arranged for her to extend her furlough for a couple months, allowing some study time at Canadian Theological College (now Canadian Theological Seminary) in Regina, Saskatchewan.

In October of 1979, Julie returned to Gabon to develop and direct a field-wide TEE program. Soon after her arrival, she had a meeting with the Bible school committee at which she presented the possibilities of TEE and how it could be incorporated into the regular Bible school training program. Her plans were accepted. Now she could get serious about getting study groups going and preparing materials for them.

Julie spent most of the next three months at her desk getting all the administrative details established—the curriculum, various certificates and diplomas, the grading system, etc. All the while, she was quietly promoting TEE to other missionaries and national pastors.

Julie looked through some old files locked up in the library of the closed Bible school. Among other things, she found a file with an 18-page report labeled "TEE." It detailed all the reasons—cultural, financial, sociological—why TEE would never work in Gabon!

This is not very encouraging, thought Julie as she sat in the dusty library, ignoring the lizards as they scampered along the walls. *OK, Lord,* she prayed. *Just in case I thought I was going to get TEE going in this country, I now give it entirely to You. If it works, You're going to get the glory for it. If it doesn't work, we just won't tell anyone.*

Julie knew the program couldn't start with a big bang. The Tsogo have a proverb that says, "Intent on attracting *étsué* (ATE-soo-AY) fish? Don't make waves." That described fairly well the tone and progress of TEE/Gabon in those first few months.

One of the first TEE students explained to Julie how the *étsué* are caught. "To catch *étsué* fish, you match cunning with cunning," he said. "*Étsué* avoid nets and fish traps. It's best to lie in wait for them with extreme patience. Even tidbits of food do not entice them. But they love company. Slowly slip your hand into the water and move it as a fish moves. Gradually the *étsué* will sidle up to your hand. Don't make a grab for it though. Just keep on being another fish and slide your hand along its fins and then enclose it in your grasp. That is *real* fishing."

Julie smiled as the man handed her a string of fish as a gift. His story accurately described the goal of TEE: to disciple mature students of the Word into becoming fishers of men, without them leaving the waters where the *real* fishing is. Like *étsué* fishermen, Julie and others hoped that by quietly doing the extension program, people would see the product and the program would sell itself as a viable way to train pastors and lay leaders.

One of the first steps was to try to interest pastors in taking courses. Julie could see the potential problem of them feeling threatened later on when laypeople became well-qualified in what had previously been the pastors' private domain—Bible knowledge. Pastor Joel and three lay leaders in the Guevede church were among the first to enroll in a TEE class. They met with Julie every week for a quiz and time to discuss together what they had been learning. The course was called, "Prayer—Conversing with God."

Over the years, Tsogo believers had been afraid to pray for others by name, believing that by doing so they called down trouble or placed a curse on those they named. In the lessons they learned that when you pray for an unbeliever, you are asking for a good thing to happen to them, not a curse.

All four students in the class recorded names in their prayer diaries of people they were praying for. Some of those named before God showed up in church one Sunday a few weeks later. Prayers were being answered.

In its second year of operation, there were eight missionaries involved in TEE working with 80 students. And there were more asking for classes. TEE was growing faster than Julie had expected in spite of all the things working against it.

Fishing by the *étsué* method was paying off.

16

"Air Canada"

Question: "What is white, comes zooming into Guevede, refuels, does maintenance, loads passengers and baggage and zooms out again?"

Answer: "Air Canada!"

That was the nickname the young people came up with for Julie and her new truck shortly after she got going with Theological Education by Extension. Her new job description kept her on the road much of the time, meeting with other missionaries and helping them get their TEE classes started. Even when she was not helping others she was away three days each week teaching her own classes in neighboring towns. And always, the vehicle was loaded down with passengers and their luggage going to visit relatives along the way. Not infrequently her passengers would change their minds after arranging to "fly" Air Canada. So if they weren't around when she was ready to leave, she didn't worry about them.

That prompted a sequel to the first riddle. "What takes off on schedule, frequently leaving passengers behind?"

Answer: "Air Canada," of course!

Julie probably kept the most regular schedule in the whole country! And people knew that if they missed their ride, they could catch the next "flight" out in a few days!

Air Canada's "plane" was a new Toyota four-wheel-drive bought with funds donated by people in North American churches. As money trickled in, Julie decided on the vehicle she was going to order. It needed to be ordered early, since it would take several months to be shipped to Gabon. When she contacted the Toyota office in Libreville, she found out that the model she wanted would be available very soon. In fact, there was one already in port, just waiting to clear customs. It could be hers.

Julie planned a trip to Libreville with two purposes in mind. One was to pick up her new vehicle. The other was to take part in the inauguration of TEE/Libreville, where 10 students were studying with missionary Roland Bowman.

She arrived in town on a Tuesday. The next morning she spoke with the Toyota dealer and found out her vehicle had just cleared customs and they were busy finalizing the paperwork. By Friday it had made it to the dealer's lot, but could not be moved until the papers came through from customs.

Nothing happened with the paperwork on the weekend as all concerned offices were closed. Nothing much happened on Monday either while everyone was getting over the weekend! Tuesday was spent getting ready for Wednesday which was a political holiday. Celebrations consumed all of Wednesday and Thursday. Friday was a day for recuperation and then it was time for another weekend!

It was a good thing Julie brought a lot of work along to occupy her days. When she wasn't running back and forth between the Mission guest house and the Toyota dealer, she had lots of TEE preparation and planning to work on. She also sat in on the two TEE classes in far-flung neighborhoods of the city. It was exciting for her to see who the students were and to hear the kinds of questions they asked and matters they brought up for discussion. All of them were either young professionals or students at the university—the kind of students that were not being attracted to the resident Bible school in the interior.

At last Julie made a successful trip to the Toyota dealer and drove off the lot in her brand new vehicle. It even had air conditioning, which made driving almost fun even in Libreville, which has more cars than streets. Julie was not a city girl and was more than ready to leave the rat race and head back to the peace and quiet of her jungle—kerosene lamps and all! And what a treat to arrive at the next stop not feeling hot and sticky and not covered with red dust from having the windows open the whole way!

Back in Guevede, Julie was loading up for her weekly trip to N'Dende, 78 kilometers (52 miles) away, when Mama Esther called out to her.

"Monyepi, bring your *gésambi* over here and I'll help you make a worthwhile load of it." (A *gésambi*, you'll remember, is the back-basket carried by Tsogo women, supported by straps over the shoulders and one around the forehead. It is part of womanhood in Gabon—a woman and her *gésambi* are not readily separated.) And what a *gésambi* Julie had! What other basket could carry cases of food, containers of water, boxes of books, firewood, seven people with their luggage and its owner as well?

Every Monday Julie loaded up her "Air Canada *gésambi*" and drove the two hours to N'Dende for her TEE class. She felt a particular burden for two store managers there who she knew were believers but were from a different tribe so were not able to understand much of the church services. Julie wondered if the upper-class people in N'Dende might be interested in a TEE class. So, on two different occasions when she was passing through, she stopped by to see the pastor, but found no one at home. It looked as if TEE in N'Dende was going to have to wait until the next term.

A few weeks later, however, Julie got a letter from a fellow missionary who ran the Christian bookstore halfway between Guevede and N'Dende. The letter said that a group of people from N'Dende had bought TEE books and wanted someone to come and work with them.

Julie made another trip to N'Dende. She learned about three men who were setting aside one day a week for Bible study, prayer and fasting for the town of N'Dende. For three months they had prayed that God would begin a revival, not with the illiterate villagers, but with themselves—the upper-class civil servants, teachers, hospital personnel, etc. One of the answers to their prayers was the 20 professionals who were already in a Bible study, many of whom were anxious to study TEE.

It was decided that there would be a Monday evening class for professionals and a Tuesday morning class for women. Julie would stay overnight in an extra room in the pastor's house. And so it was that "Air Canada" started making weekly flights to N'Dende.

Theological Education by Extension in Gabon grew much faster than Julie had anticipated. And it became a sought-after tool for training lay leaders in the church. As more missionaries became involved and more TEE centers sprang up, Julie began to spend more and more time on the road and less and less time in Guevede.

TEE started to catch on in the other French-speaking African countries in which The Christian and Missionary Alliance works. Julie soon found herself in the unofficial position of coordinator of TEE for all of these fields. Then a letter came from Alliance headquarters asking her to help organize training seminars for the other African fields. She accepted the challenge. It was a different kind of work—traveling outside of Gabon and working with church and mission leaders. It was frightening, but at the same time exciting to see what God was doing.

For someone who never had any desire to travel, Julie sure had been given a strange job! She would never have dreamed that one day she would spend so much time living out of suitcases. In her days at the University of British Columbia she thought that perhaps she might like to teach in northern Canada someday but that was about as far as she ever thought of going. And now here she was becoming a luggage specialist on the other side of the world and literally living up to her "Air Canada" nickname!

But there was a serious complication in all this travel—unless she was behind the wheel, Julie suffered from motion sickness. It was very humbling to arrive at a seminar trying to look poised and ready to teach after losing her lunch en route! "How much of a coordinator for TEE/Africa can I be when I can't even coordinate my own insides?" she often asked, only half in jest.

This was not something new. When she was a child, if anyone was going to get motion sickness on a family outing, it would be Julie. She could be counted on to perform right on cue about halfway to wherever it was they were going!

Julie's problem was not limited to travel on roads. Aboard the ship that carried her from France to Gabon in 1965, she soon learned that she also got motion sick on water. Her stomach rolled with every wave for two weeks.

Air travel resulted in a similar scenario. When a plane was at 30,000 feet, Julie's stomach was usually at 30,001 feet! She kept the suppliers of air sickness bags in business!

Julie knew before she started her new job with TEE that it would require the use of a lot of motion sickness pills and air sickness bags. On tour during her furlough before diving into TEE, Julie asked people to pray for her, that God would heal her from this plaguing problem. After all, He had created her. Could He not enable her to travel with a stable stomach?

Months later, Julie was enjoying a morning flight across Gabon as she viewed the tropical rain forest below. From a few thousand feet in the air it looked like a massive field of multi-green parsley. Then she glanced at the magazine in the seat pocket in front of her. Suddenly, she realized what she was doing. In her motion-sickness days she could not read, write, eat, move, admire scenery, think or do anything else that might upset her fragile balance during a flight. And now she was reading a magazine and enjoying the view as the plane came down through the clouds and bounced around in the after-effects of a morning rain storm. She knew that God had touched her. She wished her brothers and sisters could be there to see how "normal" she had become.

As director of TEE in Africa, Julie received an invitation to visit Guinea and help set up a TEE program there. She scheduled a stop in Côte d'Ivoire on the way.

For four days in Abidjan, Côte d'Ivoire, she was in and out of the back seats of taxis and other vehicles, swerving their way through African traffic. *This trip is going to test my healing once and for all*, Julie thought, vividly recalling her past bouts with motion sickness.

Later, returning to Abidjan after a few days up-country, Julie felt a little uneasy boarding as the 64th passenger on a 63-passenger bus. She'd forgotten her motion sickness pills. It was a beautiful new bus with 12 stereo speakers mounted in the ceiling at regular intervals. Julie's seat was directly under one of the regular intervals! And besides, that regular interval was only three seats from the back of the bus. There would be no avoiding the swing and sway as the coach cruised down the paved highway. Four hours later, Julie got off the bus in Abidjan, happy and hungry, thankful to God for her good health.

Traveling on to Guinea, Julie discovered roads worse than those in Gabon. She hadn't thought it possible! She spent three busy weeks teaching TEE seminars. The Guinean church was very responsive and quickly saw how TEE could be an integral part of their ministry in leading believers into maturity and service. She was invited to return and help them train the course leaders. It was a beneficial and encouraging time.

On the flight back to Gabon, the stewardess announced that "slight turbulence" was ahead. It turned out to be more than "slight," yet Julie enjoyed her in-flight meals with a steady stomach. To celebrate her healing, she took the motion sickness bag out of the seat pocket and began a letter on it to one of her prayer partners back in Canada. Since the bags are included in the price of the airline ticket and she was entitled to use them, she thought she'd elevate them to a new plane of usefulness!

That bag became the first of many air sickness bags Julie sent back to Canada while enjoying sickness-free flights.

17

A Country Girl in the City

Above Julie's desk hung a sign which defined a missionary as "someone who does too many things, too thoroughly, for too long." She kept it there as a reminder that she wanted to train Gabonese people to guide TEE classes and to replace her in what she was doing. She didn't need to be afraid of losing her job. The kingdom of God was big enough to supply an endless number of exciting ministries.

Julie was becoming convinced in her heart that it was time to move on. In order to coordinate TEE for Gabon and five other countries, it made good sense that she be located in Libreville rather than an isolated village in the interior. She didn't want to leave Guevede and the Tsogo people she loved so dearly, but she knew she had to. Missionaries had lived with them for nearly 40 years and the church was well established. They had a very capable pastor and they had the New Testament in their own language (though they still had only a few mimeographed copies, since the printed ones had not yet arrived from Hong Kong). It was no longer essential for them to have a missionary living there.

But in her heart, Julie was fighting the move to Libreville. She'd spent nearly 20 years in the bush. She was not city material. She loved trees, not asphalt!

It was a bright morning on the Guevede hill. Steam rose from the jungle as the sun warmed the morning air. Julie sat with a cup of coffee and opened her Bible. She paused for a moment listening to the song of the kingfisher and then resumed reading where she had left off the previous morning. She got as far as the third verse in the second chapter of Deuteronomy. "You have made your way around this hill country long enough; now turn north." Those words, directed at Moses, could have been written for Julie. She knew they were a confirmation that she had finished what God had called her to do in the hill country of the Tsogo people of south Gabon. He was now calling her to move north to Libreville.

But first there was a period of ministry scheduled for the eastern part of the country. Then there was furlough, followed by a year of study at Wheaton (Illinois) Graduate School, where Julie hoped to complete a Master of Arts degree in communications.

While she was under a pile of books and assignments in Wheaton she received letters from missionary colleagues as well as Tsogo believers telling her that the printed copies of the Getsogo New Testament had finally arrived. The eight mail sacks had been lost for two years somewhere between the Hong Kong printer and the Guevede church! The letters told of the excitement as Pastor Joel stood in front of the congregation with his face beaming and opened the boxes of New Testaments. There was special music and much rejoicing.

Seventeen years had passed since Julie was first confronted with the possibility of translating the New Testament into Getsogo. And now it was finished. Tears blurred her vision as she read the letters over and over. She would have loved to have been there to share in the festivities. Instead, she had her own little celebration of praise in her Wheaton apartment.

In July 1985, Julie returned to Gabon to begin ministry in Libreville. She was afraid. In the jungle she was well-known and respected. She knew many people and understood their ways. But in the city the people were well-educated. Many of them had traveled overseas and had good jobs. They seemed satisfied with their lives. Julie felt inferior. How could she talk to these people about Jesus? Who was she that they would listen to her? How could she love them and not be afraid of them?

The next month Julie made a trip inland to Guevede to pick up the belongings she had stored there.

The quiet, the jungle, the bird songs—it was all more beautiful than she remembered it being. She lit a fire in the living room fireplace. Her eyes followed the flickering flames, but her mind was years away. She was flooded with memories of all the times she sat in front of that same fireplace, crying out to God in the midst of aching hurts and incredible inner pain, especially during the first few years when the solitude had been so hard to handle.

But Julie knew her job there was done—it was over. The trip "home" to Guevede and the memories it triggered gave Julie strong hope for her adjustment to the city. God had not changed, but He wanted her to change. She realized that He was more concerned about the servant than the service. She might not like it in the city, but things would happen there to make her into the woman she needed to be. God, the Potter, had more work to do on Julie's character, and Libreville was the studio in which the changes would be made.

A few days after she moved into the house she shared with first term missionaries Joy Corby and Becky DeBerry, Julie chuckled at the Lord's incredible sense of humor. He was giving her large doses of village life right outside her bedroom window. Their house was in a middle-class squatter section of town, where people put up simple wooden shacks wherever they chose. The neighbor's village-style kitchen, complete with crowing roosters, was just three meters (about 10 feet) from Julie's window. At times the rooster's crow barely pierced the noise of good old-fashioned family/clan fights happening in the same kitchen!

The neighbors on the other side often hosted a men's secret society meeting—just like out in the village. The whole yard would become full of people dancing and drumming and doing their mystical ceremonies—and consuming cases of beer and wine. Julie had heard it many times before, but usually at the far end of the village. Now it was next to the wall of her house—loud and clear!

A midday rest was hard to come by. Between the secret society on one side and the women sitting on their low kitchen benches on the other, visiting and yelling at their children, Julie could only close her eyes and laugh.

The city, with all its modern conveniences, didn't make daily business much less time-consuming than it had been in the bush. She did have a computer on which to generate materials for her classes, for which she was grateful. And she also had a photocopier to reproduce materials for her students. She definitely did not miss the painstaking hours of typing stencils to be mimeographed. But she did have reservations about the wonders of the electronic age.

The photocopier broke down. Nothing serious—only a burned-out lamp which could easily be replaced. Easily replaced? Julie visited every electronic shop in the city, but to no avail. Libreville did not have a replacement lamp for the photocopier. One would have to be ordered from France.

The supply depot in France sent the wrong one, which was sent back. That was July. Everyone goes on vacation in France for the month of August, so Julie's order sat without attention for another four weeks. Then she received word that the lamp was not available in France. When all else fails, go to the source! The light bulb was eventually ordered directly from Japan!

Meanwhile Julie was preparing materials for new TEE courses for the next trimester. The "How to Preach" course needed to be sent to other African countries as well. Things were piling up.

Julie took her dog for a walk along the beach. It was something she often did to get some exercise and to release some stress. As she walked along, she turned all the hassles over to the Lord again, reminding herself that the photocopier, the course, the whole program and her time were all His. Speaking of time, she looked at her wrist to see how long she had been gone. That didn't help because her watch was broken too!

Another wonder of the age Julie discovered in Libreville was the annual road test for her car, along with several other official papers that had to be updated regularly. The road test was required for every car over a year old. In the bush, one just had to go to an office and get a paper filled out, but in Libreville the system was far more complex.

Being new to this routine, Julie asked a TEE student who worked for the Roadworthy Car Association what steps she needed to follow.

"There are three steps," he explained. "First, you pay your fee" (equivalent to seven dollars).

"Where do I do that?"

"Behind City Hall are some buildings." Julie nodded, thinking she knew the buildings to which he was referring.

"Step two," the instructions continued, "you take your receipt and car registration card to the Ministry of Transport, second floor, and make an appointment."

"Where is the Ministry of Transport?"

"Beside the new mosque. You know where that is, don't you?"

Julie nodded.

"Then step three, take your car to the public works yard at the appointed time. The public works yard is behind the Electro-Hall." She knew where that was. Electro-Hall was becoming her second home since that's where her photocopier had been purchased.

The next morning, Julie set out to find the buildings behind City Hall. After only two tries, she found the right building, deposited her money and left with her lovely pink receipt.

Now off to the Ministry of Transport. Julie drove straight to it.

"Is this where I can make an appointment for a car inspection?" she asked the man behind the reception desk.

"Yes, it is. But we do not take appointments today."

"What day do you take appointments?"

"Yesterday and tomorrow."

"May I make an appointment for tomorrow?"

"No. For tomorrow you have to come here tomorrow."

"Thank you," was all Julie could say that she wouldn't later regret. She left the office, shaking her head.

Day two. Julie returned to the Ministry of Transport, second floor. She showed the appointment man her pink receipt.

"We're all booked full for today," he told her. "You'll have to come for an appointment next week."

"This can't be happening!" Julie said, not yet losing her patience, but fearing it could happen at any moment.

"It can't?" the man replied with a questioning look. "Well, let's see. Are your papers in order? Have you paid your annual tax and got the sticker?"

"No. Where do I do that?"

"In the buildings behind City Hall." Well, at least Julie knew where that was! "Have you had your headlights checked and adjusted?" the man continued.

"No. Where do I do that?"

"At a Total gas station."

"Thank you." *Oh, to be back in the bush!* Julie thought as she left the office.

Day three. Julie confidently made her way through the building behind City Hall to the office where she'd acquired her pink receipt. Wrong office once again! She was directed to another office in another building. A record four minutes after finding it, she was relieved of her $170 road tax money and left with her peach-colored windshield sticker.

Passing a Total station on her way home, Julie stopped to see if they would do a headlight inspection. Yes! Two minutes and $3.50 later, she was handed an official little paper. "But don't you need to inspect the headlights and adjust them?" she asked the attendant.

"Oh, you want the headlights adjusted? Well, you have to come back at night for that. But we close early, so make a special appointment and come back." Julie was going to be in TEE class at 6:30 when it got dark, so she presumed her headlights were where they should be and just settled for the paper.

Day four and five were the weekend.

Day six. Julie was now ready for step two of obtaining her annual road test. She went back to the now-familiar office on the second floor of the Ministry of Transport. Yes, it was a day for making appointments, but they were full up for the day. Julie couldn't believe it. Did people sleep in line there and hit him at 8:30 in the morning for an appointment? Or, more likely, did they pay him for an appointment? Well, she wasn't about to do that, so she just hung around the office for awhile, looking out the window.

"What day should I come back?" she finally asked, heading toward the door.

The appointment man shuffled a few papers, stamped one of them and handed it to Julie. She had an appointment for 2:30 that afternoon.

At 2 o'clock Julie found her way to the Public Works yard. She knew she was in the right place when she saw all the cars and taxis lined up. To Julie's surprise, the line moved quickly. Soon it was her turn. They did a thorough inspection under the hood, checking off each item as they made their way down the list. She passed the inspection and was told to return the next day to pick up her road test certificate.

In the next 15 business days, Julie made 12 visits to the Ministry of Transport office. Her papers had been lost. One morning she spent three hours going from office to office, helping the employees look through mountains of papers trying to find the ones for her car. *If someone set fire to this city*, Julie thought as she opened yet another cupboard jam-packed full of papers, *I'm sure it would burn for five years just on stored-up paperwork!* It was beginning to strike her funny. She could hardly keep from laughing at how ridiculous the whole thing was, but she didn't dare laugh since the poor workers she was helping were all so serious about it.

After three hours of searching, Julie's papers were still not found. Then, just before leaving for lunch, the woman in charge of the office sat down and filled out new forms with Julie's name and car information. They were officially stamped. Julie left the office, having successfully acquired her road test certificate for the year.

Christmas was approaching, and Julie received a green notification card in her mailbox—there was a parcel to be picked up. She made her way to the brand-new postal complex designed to handle only parcels. The marble building was a showplace of awesome architecture and poor planning.

After waiting in line, Julie handed her green card to the lady behind a steel-rimmed, bulletproofed glass counter, who pulled her package number out of the computer to ensure it conformed to the number on the card. She waved Julie on to the next porcelain-countered window where a lady hand-copied the information from the green card to a blue card, which Julie signed. She then showed her identity card and paid $2.50 for post office expenses (someone had to pay for all those color-coded cards).

With paperwork complete, Julie crawled through the "oversize package" delivery hole under the counter to get into the entry-less customs officials' cubicle. She watched while a uniformed officer undid the brown wrapping on her Christmas gift and then slid his broken razor blade through the pretty paper.

"I don't suppose it contains a dangerous object," he said. "However, my blade did hit something hard, so I'd better check this out!" Out of the box came a bottle of perfume. So much for the fun and suspense of opening that one! The official then carefully rewrapped the package because the law said all packages must leave the elaborate new building intact.

Julie made her way back through the crawlway under the counter, through which everyone must pass in order to get to and from the customs office. This was the third time she'd done this in three days!

Julie was glad she wasn't in Libreville just to make money, which is what brought most of the other white people there. She wouldn't do it for money. But the Almighty God had called her to be there. In that she found true joy.

18

To Leave or Not to Leave?

It was September 24, 1987. Julie woke up at 6 a.m. *Why so early?* she thought. *This is my day to sleep in.* She turned away from the barely light window to give sleep another try. But every rooster in the neighborhood was busy scolding every other rooster. The day had begun.

Julie got up, had a shower and had just sat down with a cup of coffee and her Bible when there was a knock at her door. It was her friend, Blossom.

"Happy Birthday, Julie!" Blossom gave Julie a hug and a kiss and went over to the table. "I've come to have breakfast with you." She proceeded to empty the contents of her basket—a thermos of coffee, fresh fruit and croissants and place mats on which she had embroidered Julie's name.

Julie was now glad she had wakened early even though she deserved to sleep in. After all, it was her 50th birthday. And she didn't mind anybody knowing her age. The way she saw it, she was thankful to God for every year He had given her. She didn't want to pretend it was any less.

Besides bringing birthday wishes, Blossom had come to say goodbye. Julie was leaving for Canada the following week. It was not time for Julie's regular furlough, but her parents were not well. Her mother had been hospitalized for heart problems. Shortly after her release, Julie's father suffered a stroke and was lying partially paralyzed in a hospital bed. Her mother could not care for herself and her brother and sister had been taking turns staying with her while trying not to neglect their own families.

Julie was torn—this was not an easy decision. Her schedule was full week after week. There were TEE classes and training seminars. There were TEE materials to be translated into French. And there was the coordination of the entire TEE program to oversee. A lot of people were counting on her to do things she would no longer be able to if she took a leave of absence.

Julie didn't want to put her ministries on the shelf. But after much prayer and weighing of pros and cons, she decided it was right for her to respond to her family's need and stay with her mother until both her parents, in their mid-80s, could get into an extended care facility—perhaps six months. But she didn't know how long it could turn out to be.

As she grappled with her decision, peace slowly came. She realized that ministry to her parents was as valid as her ministry among the Gabonese. She needed to go. Her Gabonese colleagues, who hold strongly to the importance of family, supported her decision. One student in a leadership class prayed, "Lord, we say we're being trained. Now we will discover if we really are trained. This is good for us. This is a time for us to prove ourselves."

Julie quickly made arrangements to turn over as many of her responsibilities as possible to others and fly to Canada. And now she was one week away from leaving.

Blossom was on her way shortly after breakfast, leaving Julie to start the next part of her day. She was in the middle of sorting papers in the TEE office when there was another knock at the door. It was a missionary colleague delivering a message. A Tsogo man visiting relatives in one of Libreville's suburbs had called to say that one of the Tsogo Bible teachers had died in an accident.

Julie drove across the city to find out the details and discovered that it was Enoch, her village Papa, who had died. He had fallen from a palm tree while cutting down nuts for oil. He died a few kilometers away en route to Bongolo hospital. On top of her own parents' poor health, this was a devastating blow. The tenuous reserve of strength and peace she had was shattered. She wanted so much to go "home" to the village to be with Mama Esther and the rest of the family, but she couldn't. She would have to settle for attending the wake at Enoch's son's place in Libreville that night.

Throughout the rest of the day, Julie's thoughts were often far away from what she was doing. Tears fell on the TEE files as her mind leaped from memory to memory of dear Papa Enoch and Mama Esther.

It was around their table that Julie developed an appreciation for village food. Papa Enoch was a good hunter and they nearly always had fresh game of one kind or another which Mama Esther cooked in hot pepper sauce. Julie recalled the first time she had porcupine meat at their house. She wasn't quite sure what to do when she found a little curled-up paw on her plate. She just nibbled some of the meat off the back of the little hand-like thing as though it were a criminal thing to do. And the pepper sauce was so firey she felt like she was exhaling smoke!

And then there was the time the meat wasn't as fresh as it should have been. Julie smiled as she recalled what a struggle it was to suppress a giggle as Enoch prayed: "Lord, give us the strength to eat this meal. And please keep the food down in our stomachs peacefully so that it won't bubble up all night."

Julie thought back to how Enoch and Esther always made her feel welcome in their home in Nombo and how Esther had pierced her ears like Gabonese mothers do for their daughters. "Nombo" means "warm blanket." It was a fitting name. Enoch and Esther's home there was a refuge, a warm blanket, where Julie found protection against the "cold" of sorcery.

And she had learned so much from Papa Enoch. He always patiently explained various aspects of their culture to her and answered countless questions as Julie probed to understand the Tsogo mindset. His approval gave credibility to her teaching and helped her to establish a base for translation in the City-of-Bridges. And now Papa Enoch was dead. It couldn't be true. Julie would never again sit and learn from this wise Bible teacher.

After her evening TEE class, Julie joined about 50 Tsogo people at the home of Enoch's non-Christian son. The few Christians there quietly sang and prayed and then the son grudgingly allowed Julie to speak. Though weary, she somehow summoned the strength to encourage her listeners to make the same kind of commitment to God that Papa Enoch had made.

October 1, 1987 Julie crossed eight time zones and landed at Vancouver International Airport, physically, emotionally and spiritually spent. She felt she had nothing left to give, but knew her parents needed her. She cried out to God with all her doubts and questions. As she offered Him the broken pieces of her heart, He began to mend it and replace her doubts with peace.

Julie lived with her mother whose dimmed eyes and arthritic hands would not cooperate with what she wanted them to do. She visited her father almost daily. His feet, which once challenged her to lengthen her stride, now sat on the footrests of a wheelchair.

Would she be able to return to Gabon in six months? Should she resign from the Mission? Julie didn't know. Watching the branches on the pear tree outside her window shiver in the wet snow, she was finally able to tell the Lord she was willing to stay home indefinitely if that was what He wanted her to do. Yet she still didn't know.

As winter gave way to spring, Julie felt a new peace and a fresh conviction that her work in Gabon was not finished. She asked for a one-month extension of her leave and made reservations to return to Gabon on April 30. Then as confirmation that her return to Gabon was right, on April 6 her dad was moved into a room at an extended care facility. Three days later, her mom received a room in another wing of the same facility. Julie could return, knowing her parents were well cared for.

19

A Dream Come True

Julie had a dream. She began to envision a TEE center with office and classroom space and equipment for the production of new materials.

Missionaries Paul and Jill Goodman lived on the other side of Libreville. There were two long buildings near their home that had been part of a bankrupt contractor's housing project. Paul suggested to Julie that they would make an excellent location for the national TEE office.

Julie took one look at the overgrown yard and wooden buildings in disrepair. *New missionaries don't always see all the problems involved,* she thought. If the owner could even be found and if he would be willing to rent, there would be other challenges. First, there would be the task of convincing the church and mission leaders of the validity of the need for bigger facilities and then, of course, for money to see the project through. If those obstacles were scaled, there would be hundreds of man-hours of work involved to restore the buildings to a usable condition. Then there was the nagging thought that there was probably a lot more space there than the TEE center could use. It all seemed too far-fetched. Julie decided not to pursue it.

A few months later, Paul reminded her of the empty buildings that he heard were now for rent.

"Julie, next time you're out at our end of town," he told her, "I'm going to walk you through those buildings just to let you see them. Several of the TEE group leaders have seen them and are really excited about the possibilities." Julie knew those group leaders and knew they were realists. If they could get excited about some tumbled-down wooden buildings, perhaps she needed to take a look.

This time, from the moment her eyes laid sight on them, her vision for them immediately began to grow into something bigger than just a TEE office. Hadn't several TEE students shared with her that they felt God's call on their lives for full-time ministry? And hadn't John Corby, the director of the Bethel Bible School, expressed his concern for a theological education program in the capital where city people could be trained to work in urban centers?

The Bible school in the interior of the country was once again in operation after having been closed for eight years. This was a major accomplishment for Gabon. But if the spiritual needs of a growing Church were going to be met in the future, a higher level training program needed to be established. Julie's TEE students were eager to be trained and they were ready for university-level courses. Perhaps these were pieces of a very wonderful puzzle just waiting to be put together.

The two programs could share not only the site, but work hand-in-hand to train pastors and lay leaders for the Gabonese church. The buildings could house a Bible institute during the day and double for TEE classes in the evenings. Office space would allow for both the TEE national office and administrative and faculty needs for the institute as well. As she toured the buildings, Julie knew that using all that space would no longer be a problem. Walking those beautiful hardwood floors (well, she was pretty sure they were beautiful underneath layers of paint, dust and scratches) and moving from room to room, Julie began to feel an inner peace that this was "right."

Other missionaries saw the buildings. Some caught her vision. Some weren't so sure. Even so, she was excited.

About this time the Corbys were accompanying the Bible school students on a speaking tour around the country. While in Libreville they were taken along with a few Gabonese church leaders to the faded wooden buildings with the sagging porches. Although at that point in time they were not especially attractive buildings, they began to look better and better to the little group. As the dream was shared and the vision caught, those present drew themselves into a circle and in the hot tropical sun verbalized their claim of that place for God's purposes. There was a shared feeling of confidence that this was God's plan and He would work out the details.

As John and Julie brainstormed, the "Center for Theological Education" became a reality—if only in their minds at this point. The national church had voted against establishing a Bible school in Libreville three years earlier. Apparently the timing hadn't been right because this time the vote was favorable. The impossibilities dissolved one after another. The dream was becoming reality.

The process of gaining possession of the buildings was long and slow with the greatest battle being fought in the heavenly realms. Vandals made frequent visits, complicating future restoration. With optimism that a favorable contract would be worked out with the owner in France, the TEE students scheduled a work bee. Over 90 of the 120 Libreville TEE students were there for a major clean-up of the yard and buildings. Professors and taxi drivers, executives and housewives worked side by side, hauling truckloads of garbage and debris from the premises and washing away years of dust and cobwebs.

A few weeks later the contract was finalized. These buildings were to become the home of the Bethel Bible Institute and TEE Training Center. But there was a lot of work yet to be done.

An American couple volunteered two weeks of their time and labor. Bob did the rewiring while his wife joined Julie, Jill Goodman and whoever else they could recruit in the sanding and painting department. Some of the TEE students hung doors, scraped old paint and varnish off the edges of windows and put up trim. Anyone who dared venture near the Center in those weeks put in a few hours of work as payment for a guided tour.

One of the buildings had an apartment which was designated as Julie's home. While Paul Goodman built kitchen cabinets, Julie stripped three coats of strange-colored paint off the hardwood floors in the bedroom and living room. Three electric sanders cluttered various corners of the building, but none of them worked, so it was all done by hand.

A highlight for Julie was that her tiny new apartment had a bathtub. After 25 years in Gabon, she would be able to have a bath in a tub! No more running down to the stream and lying down in the sand to get covered with water. No more heating water on the stove to fill a bucket shower, the duration of which was a maximum of two minutes. No more fighting with a broken shower hose as she did in the house she was moving out of. But a real bathtub—luxury!

John and Fran Corby moved to Libreville where John became the director of the institute, leaving the Bible school in the interior in capable hands. Following a few panicky weeks of building desks, painting and putting up shelves, waiting for the electricity to be installed and preparing lectures, Gabon's Bethel Bible Institute and TEE Center officially opened in October, 1989. Libreville's daily paper carried an article that filled the religion section on opening day. There were 12 full-time and 13 part-time students at the institute, plus over 300 TEE students throughout the country. This was in addition to 13 full-time students enrolled in the Bible school down country, studying at a high school level.

After TEE class one evening, Serge asked Julie if she would like to come home with him and meet his mother. He was concerned about the prayer cell she was attending, which was not recognized by the Church. Having accepted Jesus only a month before, Serge didn't know enough of what the Bible taught to discuss it with his mother, but he had an uneasy feeling about her group.

Serge directed Julie down an indescribable path into a lower middle-class neighborhood. After a warm welcome and several moments of introductory conversation, the topic turned to the "wonders" of the prayer cell Serge's mother attended. Julie was able to show her from Scripture why some of those practices were wrong because they did not glorify Jesus Christ.

Driving home that night, Julie was troubled. Serge's mother represented hundreds of new believers who were not receiving adequate biblical instruction. There were not enough pastors and teachers to follow them up and get them solidly grounded in the Scriptures. Many were drawn to groups with nonscriptural but spectacular practices and bounced from one miraculous high to another, hooked on phenomena and not concerned about its source.

Julie's thoughts turned to the more than 45 adults for whom there wasn't room in the TEE classes each trimester at the Avea church alone—there were not enough group leaders, nor classrooms, nor nights of the week. The task of trying to keep up with the discipling of new believers was overwhelming. For this reason it was imperative to train the more mature Christians who could, in turn, train these new babies in Christ.

This is exactly what Bethel Bible Institute and TEE/Gabon purposed, with God's help, to accomplish.

20

Hepatitis

The road was in terrible shape between Mouila and Guevede. Julie had flown from Libreville to Mouila, and missionary colleagues were taking her the rest of the way to Guevede for Christmas. It was a good thing they were going no further since the road was completely washed out a few miles further into the hills. As they plowed their way through mud and ruts in four-wheel-drive, the cassette player joyfully resounded with, "Dashing through the snow . . . !"

Julie always liked snow and, although the song turned on a bit of nostalgia, she really was quite content with the mud. She was excited about going "home" to spend Christmas in Guevede.

What a treat it was to not have anything that had to be done! As guest in the house she had lived in for nearly 18 years, all she had to do was rest and visit. She soaked up the bird songs and other natural sounds (like mice and rats running around in the eaves). No traffic, no telephone, no electricity! And it was so good to see many of her Tsogo friends and enjoy meals of wild game and other natural foods not available in the city. They still teased her about drinking her coffee black. Why would anyone who could afford cream and sugar want to drink black coffee?

Then there were the Christmas activities, including the Christmas Eve program at the church. After several songs came the presentation of the nativity play, with angel wings getting caught in the doorway and shepherds arriving at the stable before Jesus was born. The play held everyone's attention as they wondered what might happen next.

One January morning, back in Libreville, Julie woke up with a raging fever. *Malaria*, she thought as she pulled herself out of her oh-so-comfortable waterbed. She went to the cupboard and found some medication. She hated to take it because of her allergies, making the cure almost worse than the disease. While it took care of the fever, it also gave her a long night of hallucinating. After tripping in and out of reality for several hours, Julie realized she was fighting something other than malaria. A few days passed. She turned yellow. Hepatitis!

The remedy for hepatitis is total rest—weeks of it. That put all of Julie's ministries on hold.

Some were turned over to Gabonese while others were canceled for the trimester. Day after day, week after week, Julie followed the strict orders of two doctors, both TEE students, who told her to do nothing but rest. And they stopped by regularly to check up on her.

After six energy-less weeks, the day finally came when opening her eyelids didn't take all of Julie's strength. She started spending more time each day reading and sitting out on her veranda greeting the students as they came and went from the institute next door. As her strength continued to return, Julie pulled out her well-worn copy of the Royal Canadian Airforce exercise book, printed back in the days before anybody knew how to spell aerobics. She gently forced her body to do level one of chart one of page one in an effort to cooperate with the Lord in getting herself back into shape.

During her weeks of forced inactivity Julie had lots of visitors. Some of them were students who prayed for her and wondered why she wasn't instantly healed. Julie hoped that they could see that God can be glorified even *in* illness and not only *after* getting rid of illness through instantaneous healing.

One day Julie had a most encouraging letter from Serge. Serge and his wife Marie-Claire had been in Julie's first TEE class at N'Dende. He was the manager of the local government-owned chain store. A large percent of his income came from the small bar where he and his wife both served drinks.

Serge struggled with not wanting to be at TEE class. If he closed the store in the evening to come to class, he missed out on profits from the sale of alcohol. He also felt convicted when he studied the course work. He was afraid he would have to rearrange the priorities in his life if he got really serious about following Jesus. It was easier to drop the class.

Serge was still battling with his decision to drop out of TEE when the class planned a special weekend of ministry in Guevede. Since he had heard a lot about the Tsogo tribe (most of N'Dende's population were not Tsogo), Serge decided to stick with the class a bit longer.

During the weekend of ministry, each student was to give a testimony of something God had taught them. Serge took his turn like the rest. Julie spoke with him afterward.

"Why are you standing behind a counter selling drinks when God has His hand on you to stand behind a pulpit?" she asked him. "God has gifted you to preach."

Serge was not at the next TEE class, nor any others. He was not going to further expose himself to the possibility of God turning him into a preacher! Marie-Claire, on the other hand, continued to study. She and Julie frequently prayed for Serge until a few months later when Serge and Marie-Claire left N'Dende and Julie lost touch with them.

Several years had passed before Julie received Serge's letter. She sat in her rattan chair on the porch and read it excitedly. He explained that shortly after leaving N'Dende he quit his job in the store and started a taxi business because it was beginning to trouble him that he played a part in so many people getting drunk. The only Bible-believing church in their new town was a very small one of two families who met in a house. Serge and Marie-Claire joined them. They taught their discouraged brothers and sisters what they learned in TEE about evangelism. The church began to grow.

While the church grew, Serge's business didn't. He taxied too many people without charging them! All along he had been fighting what he knew inside. God was calling him and he was trying to run away. He finally reached a point where he knew he could no longer fight with God.

"Sister Julie was right," he told his wife. "God has gifted me for the ministry." His letter concluded with an invitation for Julie to attend his church the day he was to be publicly set apart for the work of the ministry.

One morning in February, Julie got up early to get to the major research lab by 7:30 a.m. She needed a final blood test to see if she really was in as good a shape as she thought she was. When she arrived she found two people sitting on the front steps ahead of her. In a short while the group grew to 10. Then to 15. By 7:45 the lab personnel came sauntering up with the keys. When the door opened, the waiting group headed for the registration window. But the receptionist didn't go to her window! Instead she went to a table by the door. The line changed directions, making Julie third from the end instead of third from the beginning.

The receptionist then made an announcement that all labs were completely out of the products necessary to process blood tests. Gabon had not paid its pharmaceutical bills in France and the suppliers refused to supply! Only other tests would be handled. The "blood" people were excused.

Some of the blood people were genuinely distressed. How could they prove to their employer that they were sick if they could not bring a piece of paper with the proper numbers and unpronounceable words on it from the lab? In Julie's case, how could she prove to her employer that she was fit to go back to work without such a paper? No doubt by the time the country paid its bills in France and the new supplies arrived, six months or a year down the line, her blood test would turn out favorably!

Julie went back to work with renewed vigor and with renewed gratitude for the exceptional health she enjoyed.

21

"How Can I Be a Missionary?"

From the uneducated to the executives, God was working in the lives of TEE students. Francois had been taking courses for two years and excelled in his study. His name stood out to Julie when she went through the records because he was highly placed in government. So when he stopped taking courses she noticed.

Even though he was absent from TEE, Julie kept coming across his name on other people's registration forms. One of the questions on the form asked students how they came to know the Lord as their personal Savior. One student answered, "My Uncle Francois Moussavou led me to the Lord." Another said, "My colleague at work, Francois Moussavou, showed me the changes Jesus could make in someone's life." Julie asked around and found out that in the two years he'd been a Christian Francois had led 50 of his friends and family members to the Lord.

But Julie was concerned about Francois. She knew he was leading a mid-week prayer cell in his home. *If he is training others,* Julie reasoned, *he should be systematically studying the Scriptures. And he also needs accountability.*

She decided to pay a visit to Francois' office on the top floor of a government high-rise. Wading through the plush carpet, she sat down across from his desk. When asked why he stopped taking TEE classes, he replied, "I am afraid if I continue in TEE the church is going to make me into a pastor and ordain me. That would ruin my ministry!"

Julie saw that he was right. If Francois were to be ordained he couldn't roam around those government halls in the same way. He wouldn't have the same relationships with the people who were in and out of his office every day. Their behavior and their attitudes would change. He would lose his effectiveness. Julie promised him the church would not try to ordain him—unless of course he should feel God calling him in that direction.

Francois resumed his studies in TEE the following term. One day he said to Julie, "I understand you come around and visit TEE students at their place of ministry. You've never visited the prayer cell that meets in our home." Julie agreed to go the next week.

She parked her four-wheel-drive down the

street and walked down the block lined with BMWs and Mercedes to Francois' house where 140 people were gathered for prayer and instruction. For the many who would not set foot in a church building, Francois was their pastor, faithfully teaching them about new life through Jesus Christ.

It brought Julie incredible joy and satisfaction to sit and rehearse in her mind what God was doing in and through some of the people whose lives intersected hers. She was amazed at the potential of an ordinary vessel submitted to the Master.

Julie was tired as she packed her books into her bag after an evening TEE class that went late. She was already letting her mind begin to relax when a group of students approached her with a question. They were young professionals and businessmen, each actively involved in local evangelism and ministry. Their question for Julie: "How can we become missionaries?"

Julie's immediate inner reaction was, *You probably just want to go to North America where the living is easy. What do you mean by "missionaries"?* Hoping her thoughts weren't showing on her face, she advised them to present their question to the church leadership.

Home in her little apartment, Julie sat and reflected on the exchange. She was horrified at the feelings that came to the surface. How paternalistic! How racist! She confessed to the

Lord the superiority that somehow allowed her to believe that North Americans had a monopoly on the great commission. Intellectually she knew that was the farthest thing from the truth, but her heart obviously hadn't received the message.

The men came back to Julie a few days later. There was noticeable discouragement on their faces as they reported the answer they had received. It came in the form of three questions, each with a presumably negative answer: "Have you ever seen a person from Africa who is a missionary?" Secondly, "We do not have enough money to properly support our pastors. How can we possibly send missionaries?" And finally, "We do not have enough trained leaders to pastor our many churches, so why would we send trained people elsewhere?"

"So now what do we do?" the men asked Julie. "We were told we are the wrong color to be missionaries." Julie felt a certain satisfaction, knowing that others also indulged in the same negative thinking.

"Was the instruction to go and make disciples of all nations in Matthew 28:18-20 written only for white people?" one of the students continued. That brought Julie's thoughts back into focus. Again she felt reprimanded.

"No, no, it certainly wasn't," she responded. Yet she had no other answer to give. She had counseled many students, showing them opportunities for involvement in their home churches and other churches throughout Gabon. Yet she had no answer for these men.

Their question haunted her mind for months.

Julie heard that the Billy Graham Center at Wheaton Graduate School in Illinois offered a missionary-scholar-in-residence program. Each year a missionary is chosen to conduct research and write the findings into a book to be published by the Billy Graham Center. The idea of several months of concentrated study intrigued her and for years she had dreamed of writing a book. So she began to seriously consider the idea.

Several interesting subjects beckoned for her attention, yet she kept coming back to that simple question put to her by her students: How does the church in a country that's been on the receiving end of missions become involved in the sending of missionaries? How were other countries doing it? She sent in a proposal entitled, *The Body with a Heart for the World*.

Several months later, in April of 1992, Julie was at a weekend training retreat for TEE leaders. It was an intense and busy weekend. Julie had a lot on her mind. She had so much to do and only one month before she was to leave for furlough. And then, to top it off, she received a phone call at 5:30 Saturday morning from her brother Ken in British Columbia telling her that their mother had just died. She remembered how, every time they parted, her mother prayed, "Thy will be done, Lord. I give her to

You for Your work and for Africa." Julie's parents were truly great prayer warriors. She knew she could always count on their faithfulness in prayer and correspondence. Even during her mother's last months, struggling with arthritis and poor eyesight, she faithfully wrote to Julie every week.

With that in mind, Julie decided the best way she could honor her mother's arrival in Glory was to be faithful to the Lord's work to which she had released her.

When the retreat was over and people were preparing to go their separate ways, Natasha asked Julie if she could speak with her. Natasha was a sharp young woman, a first-year student at Libreville's university.

"I think God wants me to be a missionary. How do I become one?" she asked.

This time Julie's inner reaction was different. God had changed her heart. She no longer felt judgmental. She longed for The Christian Alliance Church of Gabon to become The Christian *and Missionary* Alliance Church of Gabon. Yet as she tried to answer Natasha's question she hesitated. How could Natasha become a missionary? Julie didn't know.

Natasha's question confirmed to Julie the new focus she saw her life taking. She knew she had chosen the right topic for her research proposal. Whether it was accepted or not, just defining the issue had helped her sort out her own thinking on the matter.

She handed over the leadership of TEE to another, feeling she had done with it what the Lord had given her to do. It was now up to the Gabonese to carry on. Julie didn't want to resume TEE leadership in a year or two when she would return to Gabon. In fact, she wasn't even sure she would return. Her burden for Gabon was lifting. Her new burden for making missionaries would likely take her elsewhere.

Two weeks before she left on furlough, Julie made a quick trip back to Guevede to say goodbye to her Tsogo "family." Standing on the Guevede hill, her eyes took in the beauty of the tree-blanketed terrain. Her mind leaped from memory to memory, rehearsing the highlights of many years in just a few moments. How she loved the isolation of the jungle that had once made her ache with loneliness.

There was a finality in her heart about leaving the people she loved and the land she loved. It wasn't like other furloughs when she was sure she'd be back in a year. She felt a lump in her throat and tears in her eyes as she watched the women file into the living room of the pastor's house later that evening, carrying bowls of food on their heads for her farewell feast. After the meal they gave her traditional gifts of a live hen and a stalk of bananas and a not-so-traditional gift of money.

She was going to miss these people. Yet she also knew that the Lord who had been with her in the jungle would still be with her in the unknown that lay ahead.

22

Around the World in 81 Days

The phone call came in January 1993. Julie was invited to be the Billy Graham Center's missionary-scholar-in-residence for the 1993-1994 term. What an incredible honor! She was the eighth person and the first woman to hold the position.

When her furlough year was over, Julie packed her belongings into her car and drove from Abbotsford, British Columbia to Wheaton, Illinois. As soon as she got moved into her windowless and distraction-proof office in the Billy Graham Center library, she got to work. She read everything she could find on local churches in developing countries being involved in missions. There wasn't a lot—she was treading into an area in which little research had been done. And she didn't know how to do this kind of research. What had she gotten herself into?

Julie contacted leaders of churches around the world and planned a research trip. One of the countries she planned to visit was Brazil. She got the name of a pastor of a missions-minded church from São Paulo who was visiting in the United States. Rev. Queroz (KEY-rose) was very enthusiastic about Julie's project and in his lively Portuguese accent he recommended five or six churches he felt she should visit.

She thanked the Lord that for the time being she could use English on the Brazil project, but wondered how she was going to locate a bilingual English-Portuguese person who would help her translate the surveys and questionnaires she would need in Brazil. *Julie, take it one problem at a time,* she told herself on her way to the Wednesday noon prayer meeting.

Since the prayer meeting was in the chapel on the main floor of the Billy Graham Center, it wasn't unusual for guests to attend. A woman Julie had never met before came and sat down beside her. The newcomer spoke to her in what Julie immediately recognized as "Queroz English."

"I am new in town," she began. "I'm from Miami. Well, actually, I'm from Brazil. I'm not Spanish though. I only speak Portuguese and English. My husband got a job for an international organization which moved us here from Miami. I came here to look around today. I don't know why. I saw a sign that said there was a prayer meeting, so here I am."

Julie could have told Rosa why she was there, but she restrained herself, thinking it would be more effective if the Lord told her first. But Julie did tell her she was the second Brazilian she'd spoken to that day and then answered Rosa's question about why she had talked to Rev. Queroz.

"You will need someone to translate materials into Portuguese for you, yes?" Rosa asked.

"Yes, actually, I will."

"Here's my phone number," she offered. "I would be glad to help you."

For the next few months Julie continued with background reading and revision of her questionnaires. Her lunch hours were often spent in the cafeteria with international students who helped her test and refine her questions in preparation for visiting some of their countries in the new year.

By Christmas Julie still hadn't received confirmation from her contacts in India or Nigeria and she was scheduled to fly out of Chicago on January 13. Between Christmas and New Years, Julie represented The Christian and Missionary Alliance at InterVarsity's Urbana '93 missions conference. There, among 18,000 delegates, she was assigned to the same room as a missionary from Nigeria. Not only was her roommate familiar with the church Julie hoped to visit, but she had three men with her at Urbana who were from that same church. Two of them were on her list to be interviewed in Nigeria. The third was one of their missionaries being sent to Chicago's inner city. Julie got a head start on the Nigeria part of her project.

There was a pile of mail on her desk when she got back from Urbana, including a letter of confirmation and welcome from the church in India. Her prayers were answered. All the lights were green for her to spend the next 81 days visiting missionary churches in six countries on three continents.

The answers to prayer did not cease when Julie left North America. One answer to prayer followed another as she made her way from the Philippines to Singapore to India. She met wonderful people who shared their homes, their hearts and their passion for missions. She tried to record the miracles and marvels God was doing. But it didn't take long for her to lose track. Plus she knew there were numerous divine interventions of which she was not aware, so why count? She just kept going around the world, her tape recorder in her hand, thanking the Lord with each step.

Between India and Nigeria, Julie spent an unscheduled five days in Holland waiting for her Nigerian visa to be processed. But her baggage went on to Kano, Nigeria without her. Miraculously an American missionary looking after business at the airport tripped and fell into the baggage office. As he lay prone behind the counter, moaning about his skinned knee, the name on a baggage tag caught his eye. Had he entered the office upright as he had tried to do, he wouldn't have been behind the agent's counter to see that stray suitcase. He knew the baggage was likely to be in trouble if left on its own, so he offered to relieve the agent of some of the congestion behind his counter, presuming its owner would eventually turn up. A few days later its owner arrived, thankful to find her luggage in good hands.

Julie also had stops in Brazil and Argentina. For nearly three months she woke up each morning asking herself questions like: "Which greeting do I use today? Is it the exuberant Brazilian hug or the Argentine kiss-in-the-air-as-you-touch-cheeks? Or is it the Nigerian handshake? Is it in Tamil (an Indian language) or Tagalog (of the Philippines)? Or is this the week of the businesslike Singaporean 'Good morning'?" Having called up the right greeting for the day, she usually remembered where she had just spent the night and thanked the Lord (in English!) for one more good sleep. That was followed by a mental computation of other cultural cues like, *Remember, this week you are taking your shoes off at the door.* Or, *This week you are using only your right hand for anything significant.* Or, *This week you take a cloth hanky or scarf with you as a breathing mask when you work your way through hours and hours of polluted air.* Or any number of other face-saving or life-saving devices that marked each culture.

One morning Julie awoke with a start. She was supposed to catch a 7 a.m. flight for the interior and it was now 6:45! Horrors!

She was flying around the room getting dressed and trying to locate her ticket when a question occurred to her. *Why is it that I can visualize the exact layout of the domestic airport I am in such a hurry to get to?* Then she remembered—she had been there yesterday! The 7 a.m. departure for the interior was yesterday's schedule! What a relief!

Early in April 1994 Julie arrived back in Wheaton armed with 146 interviews on nearly 200 hours of tape. The fun was over. The real work was about to begin. Julie faced the overwhelming task of turning all that information into a publishable manuscript in the next three months. She had long cherished a dream of being able to write, but now that she had the opportunity to do so, the words wouldn't flow onto the page. Her thoughts were tongue-tied.

Snug in her office, computer keys under her fingers, she hesitated. She was afraid. She didn't know how to commit her thoughts to paper. Country by country, Julie knew the outlines and the theme of each case study, but it wasn't coming out right on paper.

Deadlines stared her in the face, their weight pressing heavy on her shoulders. A horrendous pile of mail that needed attention, speaking engagements to prepare for, documents to be filled out—the list went on and on. And permeating all of the other pressures was the haunting unknown of the future. She knew that the God who had taken her around the world through experiences and appointments that no human could arrange would not stop scheduling her steps at this point. But still she wondered what was next.

Every time someone asked her when she was returning to Gabon and what she would be doing there, a string of questions resurfaced in her head. She doubted that she'd go back to Gabon. Perhaps Côte d'Ivoire? Maybe even France? Or possibly teach at a seminary in North America? She had a desire to train missionaries and to motivate the African Church to be involved. And she knew of the shortage of missions training materials in the French-speaking world. Where would she fit in? What was God directing her to do? All He seemed to say was, "This is the way, walk in it, turning neither to the right nor to the left." She knew she was in the right place for the time being, but following the completion of her project, she saw only a big blank.

On April 29, 1994, Julie wrote in her journal, "Had a lovely time with the Lord this morning, letting Him minister to my insecurities for the future, my inability to concentrate . . . my pride, ego and vanity. Romans 12:1-2. I'm on the altar again, willing for His will, but still hesitant inside. I love you, Jesus."

Julie had another fear that she voiced to only a handful of people—her health. She was experiencing a lot of pain—one joint after another. She couldn't ignore it any longer, so she went to an orthopedic doctor. He put her on a pain-killing, anti-inflammatory treatment, thinking it was arthritis. The pain became bearable. But then her stomach started acting up. Maybe she was developing the allergies that ran in her family?

Julie made an appointment to see a specialist, but it wouldn't be until after she went to Toronto for the General Assembly of The Christian and Missionary Alliance in Canada. She was to speak at the opening meeting and present a paper at the pre-Assembly Missionary Conference. In the meantime she was on a strict diet in hopes that her stomach would cooperate.

Off she went to Toronto, anticipating 10 days with longtime friends and lots of rest before returning to Wheaton ready to get back to her writing.

The story, up to this point, has been told through Julie's eyes. My primary source has been over 1,500 letters she wrote to her parents, brothers and sisters during her 30 years as an Alliance missionary. In June 1994, the letters stopped. The rest of the story comes from my memory and the memories of others who were there, and from my journal of the summer of 1994.

23

Missionary to the World

I was excited about attending General Assembly in Toronto and the pre-Assembly Missionary Conference. I was especially looking forward to seeing Julie. I knew about her arthritis, but not about her digestive problems, so was surprised to see how thin she was. She did not look well.

The usual sparkle in her eyes was dulled by pain and her laugh didn't come as readily as it normally did. I suspected something was not right. In privacy the next morning, she told me about her pain and indigestion, the bloating in her abdomen and sleepless, pain-filled nights.

Julie tried to put on a brave front, attending most of the pre-Assembly meetings, and even presenting a paper in one of them. On Tuesday afternoon, June 21, in the communion and prayer service, Julie was anointed with oil and prayed over, following the pattern in James 5. Although the pain did not subside, the accompanying worry and anxiety did.

That evening Julie addressed the opening session of General Assembly, speaking of the triumphant church in Gabon. As she told the crowd how God was using vessels of clay to accomplish His work, she was very aware of her own clay vessel. In spite of the painkillers she took before the meeting, she was very uncomfortable. The medication wore off as the meeting went on and Julie's discomfort turned to pain. As soon as she could, she went back to her room and lay down for a fitful sleep.

There were people at the Assembly Julie wanted to see. She had a lot of unanswered questions about her future. At breakfast one morning with Dr. David Rambo, president of The Christian and Missionary Alliance in the United States, she shared her burden for the Church in the French-speaking world and its need to become a missionary Church. She told him of the lack of materials in French for training future missionaries. They shared some possibilities for Julie's ministry and where her gifts and expertise might be put to use when she finished her book for the Billy Graham Center.

"I think it's time we release you from being a missionary to Gabon," Dr. Rambo told her, "and free you to be a missionary to the world."

Julie also met with Dr. Gordon Smith, the academic dean of Canadian Theological Seminary. Would she teach missions at the seminary part-time while she completed her research project, he wanted to know.

It was something she would love to do—reproduce herself as a missionary. And yet the thought of pulling an entire course together in time for September was overwhelming. She knew she didn't have the strength to do it. She declined the offer. But what would she do? Where would she fit in?

Thursday morning, June 23, I drove Julie to the Missionary Health Institute where she had made an appointment to see Dr. Kenneth Gamble. He didn't think arthritis was the problem, and ordered some tests.

Friday morning Julie felt slightly better, but there was a new development. Her tongue was swollen, causing her speech to be slurred. She felt well enough to attend the morning service, but slipped out when it was over to phone Dr. Gamble and tell him about her tongue. The next thing I knew someone was calling me out of the business session that followed. Dr. Gamble wanted to see Julie again. I was to drive her to his office.

At this visit she told him more of her problem with indigestion and that she wasn't able to keep meals down. He gave her antibiotics to take care of the swollen tongue but the other symptoms caused him serious concern. He wanted to do an ultrasound but could not get her an appointment for that day. Could she extend her stay in

Toronto and have the test Monday? Since Julie's health insurance in the United States had expired, she knew it was wise to stay in Canada where her medical expenses would be covered. The arrangements were made. As we left the Missionary Health Institute that windy morning, Julie began to cry.

"I hurt so bad," she told me. "And they can't tell me what's wrong."

Saturday morning there was a buffet brunch. Julie picked at her meal, eating very little. She felt like leaving, but wanted to stay since she knew the program was to conclude with prayer for healing. Once again she was anointed with oil and prayed for. Once again the abdominal pain remained, but the aches and pains in her shoulders and other joints were gone, never to return. She knew God could heal her completely if He chose to do so. She prayed for strength to be faithful.

Sunday afternoon's finale to General Assembly was the missionary rally, always a highlight for the attendees. Julie tried to rest in the morning so she could take in the climax of the week. For much of the meeting she sat doubled over in pain, then left to return to her room.

Monday, June 27. Julie went for the ultrasound with mixed emotions. She wanted to find out what was wrong and yet she was scared that it might be very serious. The technician was concerned with what she saw and asked Julie to wait while she phoned Dr. Gamble. He wanted to examine her again.

Still unsure of the source of the pain, he explained that it could be Julie's gallbladder, but he could not rule out the possibility of cancer. He managed to get Julie an appointment with a surgeon who admitted her immediately to North York General Hospital.

Monday was also the day I flew back to Calgary where I was working for the summer. I left Toronto knowing only that Julie was in the hospital.

Tuesday, June 28. More tests. Julie was on morphine to ease the pain. It was determined that her bile duct was blocked. The doctors cleared it that afternoon.

Wednesday, June 29. Still more tests. The bloating in her abdomen was caused by nearly five liters of fluid that was drained out Wednesday afternoon. The fluid was sent to the laboratory for testing.

Thursday, June 30. *Cancer!* Dr. Gamble explained that cancerous cells had been found in the fluid but they were unsure where they were coming from. There was a good chance it was ovarian cancer, but that was not certain, and it had likely spread to other organs. Surgery was needed to determine the extent of the cancer. It was scheduled for July 5.

That afternoon Julie wrote in her journal, "Oh God, my God—I want to trust You totally . . . I don't believe this is anger I feel—just a numbness. How can I be angry at You when You've given me more than I ever expected?"

Friday, July 1. I talked to Julie on the phone. We both cried as she talked about the possibility of her death in the near future. She reminded me of a conversation we had two years earlier, the morning her mother died. As the sun came up that morning in April 1992, we imagined what we thought heaven might be like. "I may soon find out the answers to our questions," she told me. "But I won't be able to write and tell you about it."

We talked several more minutes, mostly about the various tests Julie had been through and the questions she had. At the close of our conversation she told me to go read Psalm 73:26. After we hung up I read, "My flesh and my heart may fail, but God is the strength of my heart and my portion forever." In the midst of all the unknown, Julie had a sure faith in God.

Sunday, July 3. Early in the morning, Julie wrote in her journal again. "Romans 12:1-2. For how many years have these verses guided my life? That does not change now. Even though my body is full of death cells, multiplying at their own murderous pace, this body is still a living sacrifice which I can intelligently give to the God of my life."

That evening Joan Carter, a friend of Julie's since Bible school days, arrived in Toronto to walk with her through the days ahead. She stayed with Judy Milne, the director of missionary services for the Alliance in Canada. Judy also spent as much time as she could at the hospital.

Tuesday, July 5. Julie underwent four hours of surgery for what the surgeon termed a "widespread and aggressive" cancer. He removed a large tumor from her upper abdomen, but was unable to get it all. It was a secondary tumor. He was unsure of the primary source. The prognosis was not good.

Thursday, July 7. I spoke with Julie on the phone. She recognized my voice right away, but was obviously heavily medicated. "I know God is working here," she told me, her speech slow and deliberate. "I don't know what He's doing, but He is working."

Later that day Joan Carter phoned to report that there was concern that Julie's kidneys may be shutting down. They weren't sure that she would live another day.

Julie's sister Florence flew out to Toronto, arriving that evening. Julie perked up when she saw her. They met together with Dr. Gamble who explained the seriousness of the situation. Julie could die within the next 24 hours or she could live two years or more if she regained enough strength to undergo chemotherapy. He advised that if her other sister and brothers wanted to see her, they should come to Toronto immediately.

Friday, July 8. I tossed and turned all night, waking up several times, wondering if Julie was even alive. In the morning I dialed the number for North York General and the extension to Julie's room. I could hear my heart beating as the phone rang once . . . twice . . . three times.

"Hello?" came Julie's voice over the line. She had made it through the night.

She told me she was feeling much better and was sitting up in a chair doing breathing exercises. She also told me her sister Dolores and her brothers Ken and Bernie were coming for the weekend.

Twice that day people suggested that I go back to Toronto. I talked to Joan who asked Julie if she wanted me to come. The answer? "Yes." I made plans to return to Toronto on Tuesday, July 12 after Dolores, Ken and Bernie had returned to their homes.

Test results revealed that Julie had cancer of the gallbladder, very rare and unresponsive to treatment. When it became evident from a medical standpoint that it was unlikely she would ever return to Wheaton, Julie started recording instructions for the Billy Graham Center. She explained how far she had progressed in her project and where all her notes and resources were kept.

Meanwhile in Illinois, Dr. Lois McKinney, professor of missions at Trinity Evangelical Divinity School in Deerfield and one of Julie's project advisors, was praying for Julie while she was driving along the freeway. As she prayed, she felt an incredible sense of the Lord's presence. She knew that He was directing her to complete the writing of Julie's book.

Still somewhat hesitant, but sure she had heard from the Lord, Lois phoned a colleague. She was only part way through her story when he interrupted her.

"Let me finish the story," he said. "God told you that you will help Julie finish her book." That was the confirmation she needed. Lois phoned Julie and told her the news. Julie was buoyed, knowing that God valued her project enough to see it through to completion.

Tuesday, July 12. I flew from Calgary to Toronto where I spent a precious week with Julie. It was hard to see her so ill and yet there was no other place I wanted to be. The night before I arrived, Julie's pain was intense and she cried out to God to take her home. As we prayed together that evening, her request was that in the midst of her pain she wouldn't let Him down. Her countenance was peaceful as she affirmed that she just wanted whatever would bring the most glory to God.

I spent many hours that week rubbing Julie's swollen feet. And we talked for quite a few of those hours. She spoke of Paul's words in Philippians 1:20. "I eagerly expect and hope that I will in no way be ashamed, but will have sufficient courage so that now as always Christ will be exalted in my body, whether by life or by death." She could empathize with Paul.

Her mind turned back several years to the time she and Nyondo translated that verse into Getsogo and Nyondo related to her his experience of choosing between salt and honey. Both were good, but he couldn't have both. It would be one or the other. Julie now understood that Tsogo saying very clearly.

She talked freely of dying. She had no fear of death (though there were some concerns about the process). She knew that when her life on earth ended she would be with Jesus forever.

One morning I was reading to her from Psalm 116. She stopped me after I read verses eight and nine, "For you, O LORD, have delivered my soul from death, my eyes from tears, my feet from stumbling, that I may walk before the LORD in the land of the living."

"That is where I am going!" Julie said. "We usually talk about *this* as being the land of the living, but we've got it backward. This is the land of the dying. I am *going* to the land of the living!" Then she added with excitement in her voice, "Soon I will be able to stop talking *about* Jesus and just talk *to* Him."

Julie continued to demonstrate an attitude of thanksgiving, even when the pain broke through between doses of medication. "God is so good!" she said repeatedly. She looked at her situation and compared it to that of a Gabonese woman writhing in pain on a bark mat in a dark, smoke-filled house. She was thankful for an adjustable bed, pillows under her head, a fan to keep her cool, medication for the pain and family and friends who loved her and did what they could to make her comfortable. She was grateful for the opportunity to spend time with people she loved and to say proper good-byes. She was even thankful for the cream of mushroom soup that came for lunch. She never did like cream of mushroom soup, but managed to eat half the bowl.

When the supper tray arrived later that day, Julie lifted the lid from the bowl and once again found herself face to face with cream of mushroom soup. "I must have been too thankful at lunch time!" she quipped. Then she launched into a monologue of all the ways she liked to eat mushrooms. She loved them fresh, sliced into a salad. Or they could be fried and enjoyed on top of steak. They added flavor to any number of casseroles. Plus they reminded her of the children who came to her door in Gabon balancing baskets full of mushrooms on their curly heads. Then, taking another look at her soup, Julie wrinkled her nose and asked, "But why would anybody want to *drink* mushrooms?"

A picture came to my mind again and again through that week I spent in Toronto. As I watched the cracks in Julie's clay vessel get wider and wider, I saw the treasure inside shine through brighter and brighter. She was suffering from such a horrible disease, yet she refused to let her spirit be defeated by it. She was walking very close to the Lord she loved and was drawing others closer to Him as well. Doctors, nurses, colleagues, friends—all who came to see Julie were impacted by her consistent display of supernatural courage and peace.

Julie struggled with not being able to concentrate well enough to write. She wanted to write some notes, but lost her thoughts mid-sentence. She had always been able to communicate through paper and ink and felt frustrated that she could no longer do that.

Saturday, July 16. Julie made her last attempt at writing in her journal. She wrote some lines about death, only partially legible. Her thoughts trailed off, leaving incomplete sentences in tiny script. But the entry concludes with one clearly-written sentence. "I still have breath; therefore, I still praise the Lord."

Julie had recovered from her surgery, gaining strength and color. She had even gone on a couple short walks down the hallway and back to her room. Two weeks after her surgery she had regained enough strength to be transferred to a hospital in Langley, British Columbia, just two blocks from her sister Florence's home. Through a series of what Julie termed "mini-miracles" all the details were looked after much faster than the hospital staff expected.

Sunday, July 17. Julie left North York General Hospital alive, which a week earlier had seemed an impossibility.

While I was in Toronto the thought crossed my mind that Julie's story should be written.

Part of me clung to the hope that God would heal her. Another part of me realized that the healing I was praying for could well be her ultimate healing—that of receiving a new body upon her entrance into heaven. I knew Julie dreamed of writing her own story, but it looked like that dream would never be realized.

I voiced my thoughts to Judy Milne and Joan Carter and found out they both concurred. Julie's story needed to be written. We all agreed it should be written by someone who loved her. Joan suggested that maybe I could have a part in making that happen.

Back in Calgary, I phoned Julie every two or three days. Our conversations were short. Though she always recognized my voice, she wasn't able to concentrate for any length of time.

Tuesday, August 2. Julie was more alert than she had been in weeks. I decided to tell her that I was thinking about writing her story. After skirting around the question for a few minutes, I finally asked her, "Do you want me to write it?" I'm sure I will never forget her answer.

"Yes, I do." She took a deep breath. "You share my sense of humor . . . you share my sense of joy . . . you share my sense of beauty. There's a closeness of spirit there that makes you the one to write it."

That evening, tears streaming down my face, I committed myself to writing Julie Fehr's story.

24

"Jesus Only"

When I said goodbye to Julie on July 17 at the Toronto airport, I didn't expect to see her again this side of heaven. But the Lord had a different plan. He allowed us to spend one more precious week together at the end of August.

As soon as I was free from my responsibilities in Calgary, I headed straight for Canada's west coast and Langley Memorial Hospital. I walked into room 206 on August 23 and immediately felt the sting of tears in my eyes. I knew Julie's health had deteriorated, but I wasn't prepared for what I saw. I walked over to the bed. Julie's sunken eyes met mine. Her lips curled into a faint smile as she reached out a thin arm to grasp my hand, her watch hanging loosely halfway to her elbow. Yet still she was grateful.

"Thank You, Lord, for bringing Lisa," she whispered.

Talking was an obvious effort for her. She spoke slowly and her words were slurred. Her respiration was slow, with several seconds passing between each breath. The cancer had spread to her lungs and other organs. Her abdomen was solid tumor, blocking her digestive system. Unable to eat, Julie was literally starving to death.

Though incapable of doing the things she was used to doing, Julie's life continued to impact those around her. One nurse made a point of telling her how watching her suffer had opened his eyes. He was amazed by the peace she had because of her sure faith in Jesus Christ.

On another occasion, in the middle of the night, the intravenous needle in Julie's arm began to leak. It had to be removed and a new needle put in. It took seven tries before the nurses could find a vein that was satisfactory. I know all the pokes hurt her—I was holding her other hand and she squeezed mine with every try—but she didn't utter a word of complaint. One of the nurses commented on how well she was taking it all, to which she replied, "It's God's enabling."

Julie was on constant morphine, but received extra shots when the pain became too much to bear. The medication made her hear sounds that only she could hear and see pictures on the wall that only she could see. She was frustrated by her inability to think clearly.

"I can't believe that some people actually *pay* to feel this way!" she said, shaking her head.

Saturday, August 27. Julie's pastor and his wife, Jack and Gladys Schroeder, came to see her. Shortly before they left, Pastor Jack asked Julie if she had a message for the congregation he could pass on the next morning. She laid her head back on the pillow and thought for a moment.

"Tell them," she began, "tell them that God is love." She took a breath. "Tell them that He never changes. And . . ." she paused again for several seconds before finishing, "tell them that all that's written about Him in the Scriptures is true."

Julie didn't want to be left alone. Someone was with her all day and her sister Florence and I took turns staying the night.

Monday, August 29. Shortly after midnight Julie woke up.

"Help me! help me!" she cried. She said it felt like there was a foot in her back and asked me to call a nurse to give her a shot for the pain.

While we waited for the nurse to arrive, I sat beside Julie, holding her hand. She turned her head toward me. "Am I going to live through the night?" she asked.

"I don't know, Julie," I replied as the tears began to roll down my cheeks. "But God does know and He will decide when it's time to take you home."

She nodded.

A nurse came at that moment and gave Julie a shot. And then we were alone again.

Julie wanted to sit up on the side of the bed with her feet hanging over the edge. It was easier for her to breathe in that position. I helped her up and then sat beside her on the bed, rubbing her back.

"I still feel like I need to make a decision here," she said.

"About what?" I asked.

"I need to decide whether to live or to die." The strong medication Julie was on obviously interfered with her reasoning.

"Julie, that's not your decision," I reminded her. "The only decision you needed to make, you made years ago, and that was to follow Jesus. Your life is in His hands. It's up to Him now."

She nodded as she leaned against me. "Yes. I choose Jesus."

At that moment, the old hymn "Jesus Only" came to my mind. I recited the words of the refrain:

> "Jesus only, Jesus ever,
> Jesus all in all we sing,
> Savior, Sanctifier, and Healer,
> Glorious Lord and coming King."

For the next half an hour or more we talked about those words. "Jesus only." Jesus is the only One who can save. He is the only One we need. He was with us that night. "Jesus ever."

Julie knew she would be with Jesus forever. Her life wouldn't end when she left the physical realm. She would always be with Jesus.

We were silent for a few moments. Then I asked Julie if she was ready to get back into bed.

"No. I need to think this through again," she said. "I need to resolve this."

Again we talked about the decision of whether she would live or die being out of her hands. It was entirely God's decision and we didn't need to worry about it.

"Yes, I choose Jesus," Julie declared slowly and emphatically. "Jesus only!"

I asked her again if she was ready to go back to bed. This time she nodded. As I tucked her in, I asked her how she was feeling in her heart.

"Oh, such peace," she whispered.

I sat beside her bed that night and sobbed. Thinking she was asleep, I laid my head on the bed and let the tears flow. As I cried out to God I felt a hand on my shoulder. It was Julie's hand. She was sharing in my pain and somehow, in the midst of the hurt, I shared her peace.

That evening I was again by Julie's side. The nurses were being extra kind to me, bringing me coffee and biscuits. I had a feeling they knew it wouldn't be long. Then her doctor came to see her. He checked her pulse and looked at the dials on the machines. He took a step toward the door, then turned and said very kindly, "You know this is it? She's not likely to live through the night."

I just nodded. I suppose I already knew that, but there was some finality in hearing it from the doctor. Not long after he left, Florence came in to stay for the night, but I couldn't leave. We both stayed.

Julie woke up late in the evening. She looked at Florence and asked, "Where are we going? You lead the way."

Florence told her that it was Jesus leading the way and that He would lead her home.

"OK, Jesus. Let's go," Julie responded clearly. She turned toward us. "Don't weep for me," she said. She spent the next several minutes telling Jesus over and over that she loved Him. Florence and I began to sing hymns. Julie didn't have the strength to join us, but she encouraged us to continue singing.

Julie's speech became less and less clear and she slipped into unconsciousness. Her brother Ken came to see her. She didn't wake up. He leaned over and spoke in her ear, telling her he loved her. Julie didn't stir, but one large tear fell from her eye and rolled down her cheek.

She remained unconscious for most of the night. Just before the first light of dawn made its way through the blinds in her room, she woke up one last time. She told Florence and me again that she loved us.

"I love you too, Monyepi," I replied.

"Monyepi," she whispered. "Yes, that's what they called me—Monyepi." That name—*Beautiful One*—seemed so appropriate that morning. She had experienced so much pain. Her body was betraying her. Yet her spirit was more beautiful than ever.

Julie spoke again. The last words to leave her lips were, "Jesus only."

Nearly eight hours later, at 3:41 that afternoon, Tuesday, August 30, 1994, Julie's clay vessel broke. She left it behind and went home to be with Jesus forever.

25

"Missionaries Don't Come Any Better"

Triumphant strains of "The Hallelujah Chorus" rang through the over 2,000-seat sanctuary of Sevenoaks Alliance Church in Abbotsford, British Columbia. Yes, it was a time of mourning, but it was also a time to celebrate a life lived for Jesus. Hundreds of people gathered on the afternoon of Tuesday, September 6, 1994, to say their final goodbye to Julianna Rose Fehr. Miles of land and ocean prevented hundreds of others from joining us.

There is no way to know the number of people touched by Julie's life. But at her funeral we got a glimpse into the far-reaching extent of her ministry. Close to home, we heard of the impact Julie had on her family, as her brothers and sisters each shared special memories of their dear sister.

Among other things, Julie's brother read a poem she had written several years earlier.

Sojourney

A letter came today
Their lives go on and I'm not there
When next we meet there will be large
    chunks of their lives
Missing from mine
Homesick

Its postmark was weeks old
Weeks filled with other happenings
An ocean, a continent swallowed
    the newness
I read history
And wish

Had I been there with them
Just think of all I could have done
To lift a load, to laugh along, to
    share a sigh
Retroactive
I pray

I'll share the letter's news
Oops! Culturally we're in different worlds
When I laugh I have to explain why
    and I sigh
Letter in hand
A pilgrim

Which country am I in?
Which country did the letter leave?
It doesn't matter as the gap stretches
    both ways.
Gabon—British Columbia
Sojourney

Not only was Julie loved and respected by her immediate family, but also within the Alliance family. From the superintendent of the Canadian Pacific District, we heard that Julie had been "adopted" by more Alliance churches than any other missionary he was aware of.

A fax received from the Alliance missionaries in Gabon told of the deep loss they felt. It also told of plans to honor Julie by naming the soon-to-be-constructed TEE building in Libreville in her memory.

In another fax, Dr. Arnold Cook, president of The Christian and Missionary Alliance in Canada, noted: "Missionaries don't come any better than Julie Fehr." It went on to say, "Julie was outstanding in every way. Her quiet but effective development of Theological Education by Extension for the Gabonese Church met a very critical need. She had the confidence of the National Church leaders as few others have. She was the obvious choice to serve as the coordinator of TEE in the other West African fields."

There were also faxes from those outside the Alliance whose contact with Julie came through international conferences on TEE. Because of Julie's courage and determination, they said, a French-language TEE program had been established. Plans were already underway to adapt the materials she developed for use in Quebec and French-speaking Europe.

Following the reading of other faxes, Dr. James Kraakevik, director of the Billy Graham

Center in Wheaton, stepped to the pulpit and spoke these words:

> On June 13, 1994, the advisory committee of the Billy Graham Center missionary-scholar-in-residence met with the 1993-94 scholar, Julie Fehr. She had recently returned from her field work which took her around the world in 81 days. *The Body with a Heart for the world*—how does the local two-thirds world church become involved in global missions? That was her topic.
>
> She shared with us at that time the excitement of her project and her plans to complete it by December. She had interviewed 146 Christian leaders in Singapore, the Philippines, India, Nigeria, Brazil and Argentina to learn the secret of the phenomenal growth of missions from the two-thirds world churches.
>
> But God had other plans for this faithful disciple of His who gave her heart to Christ on the floor of a hockey dressing room in Saskatchewan at age eight. Later, as a young teacher, she responded to the Lord's call to world missions.
>
> Julie was a pioneer missionary, Bible translator, educator, international authority on Theological Education by Extension, writer, scholar—all of these. But we remember her as a Spirit-filled, gracious daughter of the King of kings—a woman of God.
>
> What describes her best for me is found in Malachi 3:16-17: "Then those who feared the LORD talked with each other, and the LORD listened and heard. A scroll of remembrance was written in his presence concerning those who feared the LORD and honored his name. 'They will be mine,' says the LORD Almighty, 'in the day when I make up my treasured possession.' "

> Julie is one of those in the Lord's book of remembrance, a choice jewel in the treasured possession. And so He has called her home.
>
> But we loved her. We will miss the joy of life that she shared with us for this past year. We thank God for Julie Fehr. She lived for His glory.

When Julie first told the Lord she would be a missionary, she added, "I want it to matter that I've lived."

That prayer was abundantly answered as attested to by those who spoke at her funeral. But we all knew it wasn't human recognition that motivated Julie. There was Another whose approval she sought more than anything else, and that Other is Jesus—Jesus only!

As the congregation stood and sang that hymn, "Jesus Only," it reminded us of the desire of Julie's heart to glorify Him. She was merely a vessel made of clay, but of outstanding use and beauty in the Master's hands.

Half an hour later, a smaller group stood in the wind beside a freshly dug grave. We cried and sang together. Then Pastor Jack Schroeder reminded us of the angel's words to Mary Magdalene and the other Mary that first Easter morning when they went to Jesus' tomb: "He is not here; he has risen, just as he said" (Matthew 28:6).

"Likewise," Pastor Jack said, "Julie is not here. She is risen!"

It was only her body—broken clay—that was committed to the ground that day. Julie Fehr is alive and without pain in the presence of Jesus Christ, the Jesus she loved.

The Jaffray Collection of Missionary Portraits

#1 *Let My People Go*
(Story of Robert A. Jaffray/China, Indonesia)

#2 "*Weak Thing*" in Moni Land
(Story of Bill and Gracie Cutts, Irian Jaya)

#3 *On Call*
(Story of Dr. David Thompson, Gabon)

#4 *To China and Back*
(Story of Anthony and Evelyn Bollback, China, Japan)

#5 *Please Leave Your Shoes at the Door*
(Story of Elmer and Corrine Sahlberg, Thailand)

#6 *A Heart for Imbabura*
(Story of Evelyn Rychner, Ecuador)

#7 *No Sacrifice Too Great*
(Story of Ernest and Ruth Presswood)

#8 *Edge of Conflict*
(Story of Harry and Miriam Taylor,
Cambodia, Philippines, Lebanon)

#9 *One Shall Chase a Thousand*
(Story of Mabel Francis, Japan)

#10 *The Promise*
(Story of Edward and Virginia Jacober, India, Israel)

#11 *Journey to Joy*
(Story of Norman and Marie Ens, Cambodia, Thailand, France)

#12 *To Vietnam with Love*
(Story of Charles and EG Long, Vietnam, Malaysia)

#13 *By an Unfamiliar Path*
(Story of David and Arlene Peters, Colombia, Brazil)

#14 *In Peril on the Sea*
(Story of Ethel Bell and her children, Robert and Mary, Africa)

#15 *A White Lady Doing Nothing in the Tropics*
(Story of Herman and Mary Dixon, Borneo)

#16 *Both Feet on God's Path*
(Story of Julie Fehr, Gabon)